WO

ARCHITECTS IN PR
Series Editor:

G000078138

Sir Reginald Blomfield
by Ginsbury, *c.* 1906

SIR REGINALD BLOMFIELD
An Edwardian Architect

Richard A. Fellows

A. ZWEMMER LTD
LONDON

Published by A. Zwemmer Ltd
26 Litchfield Street London WC2

ISBN 0 302 00590 0

Series designer: Christine Charlton
Made and printed by BAS Printers Limited,
Over Wallop, Hampshire

Cover illustration: Moundsmere Manor,
Hampshire (34).

Acknowledgements

All illustrations are reproduced from
material in the author's collection. The
following are reproduced by courtesy of the
Commonwealth War Graves Commission
(98, 99, 100); *Country Life* (25, 26, 28, 29,
44, 45); Macmillan (illustrations by
F. Inigo Thomas, from *The Formal
Garden in England* 17, 18, 19); Mr and Mrs
John Ryan (frontispiece).

CONTENTS

PREFACE

Reginald Blomfield was not a shy or retiring man. Throughout his long career he constantly made his feelings known about current issues in architecture, and he was always eager to contribute to debate. As a result, his name frequently appeared in reports and articles in the professional press, and occasionally in national newspapers. Later in life, particularly, he seems to have been considered a 'newsworthy' figure, and his buildings and books received copious reviews. There is, therefore, no lack of material with which to begin a study, although there are a few frustrating gaps in recorded information which prevent the composition of a complete picture. Blomfield's *Memoirs*, however, present an overall view of most of his life which can be used as a basis for further investigation.

Blomfield completed *Memoirs of an Architect* in 1932, about ten years before his death. Their existence is something of a mixed blessing for the researcher, because although they give very clear hints about the character of their author, there is always a temptation to use them uncritically. The *Memoirs* are a personal record and events may be distorted when seen from a single point of view. Nevertheless, they have been drawn on frequently in the preparation of this book, partly because they provide a précis of complex occurrences and partly because it is almost impossible to resist the temptation to use the author's own pithy, stylish phrases. His other books have also been valuable, not only as a guide in tracing the development of his ideas, but also because his general attitudes show through so clearly. Volumes often contain personal reminiscences and reflections, such as the short biography, *Richard Norman Shaw, RA*, published in 1940. Here, for instance, a section deals with fellow members of the Shaw 'family', whom Blomfield knew as young men, before they went on to become distinguished practitioners. Direct reminiscences about Blomfield himself are not so easy to come by, but may be found, for example, in the autobiography of C. H. Reilly, *Scaffolding in the Sky* (1938), and in his book *Representative British Architects of the Present Day* (1931).

Blomfield's buildings are generally well represented in the architectural press, particularly after the mid 1890s. Reviews contain photographs, plans and descriptions, but often centre around perspectives produced, for instance, for Royal Academy exhibitions. Several of these still exist and are to be found in the RIBA Drawings Collection in London along with a set of sketch books, photographs and other documents. The collection is by no means complete, however, and the architect is known to have disposed of drawings during the early years of the Second World War. A few packets only escaped, to be found some thirty-five years later. Nevertheless, most of the larger buildings were adequately illustrated in magazines and journals.

Although Blomfield was himself a fine draughtsman, he often employed others to make perspective drawings in their own manner, certainly after the turn of the century. Notable among artists were James B. Fulton (died 1922), Adrian Berrington (1887–1923) and Stanley D. Adshead (1868–1946). In the inter-war years Cyril A. Farey (1888–1954) was frequently employed.

Apart from the items at the Drawings Collection, there is no centralised archive of documentary information in the sense that, for instance, Lutyens' letters are catalogued and kept by the British Architectural Library. Correspondence by Blomfield can be found within other collections, as can be seen from the bibliography to this book (p. 175), but it usually concerns isolated topics so that few themes can be followed through. There are also manuscripts in the possession of the family, along with certain business documents. Blomfield kept press cuttings as a record of reviews and reports, but they were stored loose and not formalised into a scrap book. A very valuable source which is not available to the general public is the unpublished 'Epilogue, 1932–1942', completed in March 1942, a few months before Blomfield's death. To some extent, it carries on from where the *Memoirs* leave off. In his preface Blomfield says that 'this book is strictly confidential and is not to be published. It may be useful some day for reference in order to correct erroneous versions of facts and personalities but its purpose is really cathartic.' I have respected this wish, and have allowed the 'Epilogue' to inform some of my comments both about events and the author himself, but I have avoided direct quotations and have not used any information which is a matter of opinion rather than fact.

I must thank Blomfield's granddaughter, Mrs John Ryan, for access to the 'Epilogue' and other documents and, indeed, all the members of the Blomfield family who have offered assistance, especially Mr Giles Blomfield. In the early days of research Dr Walter H. Marmorek was kind enough to allow me to examine his offices in New Court, Temple, for remnants of Sir Reginald's occupancy, something that met with a measure of success in the retrieval of drawings and photographs. I should also like to thank the many county archivists, librarians and clergymen who have answered my queries, and the owners and occupants of some of the buildings mentioned in the text who have generously allowed me to inspect their property.

Margaret Richardson and other staff at the RIBA Drawings Collection have gone out of their way to offer help and advice over a long period of time on a variety of matters. Academic advice, specifically, has come from Dr Derek Linstrum and Dr Jeremy Taylor of the Institute of Advanced Architectural Studies, University of York, and Dr Peter Willis of Newcastle University. Finally I should like to include in my thanks all those who have, in any way, made my task easier.

Richard A. Fellows
June 1984

INTRODUCTION

The Edwardian period in British architecture was a time of richness and complexity, encompassing a wide variety of styles and approaches to design, and notable for the wealth of talent and inventiveness of its architects. Sir Reginald Blomfield (1856–1942) was one of its most significant figures. His career began in the penultimate decade of Queen Victoria's reign, when the brilliant Richard Norman Shaw was the outstanding influence in architectural design, and lasted until the end of the 1930s, by which time the ideas of the Modern Movement had become well established. He was prominent in a wide variety of activities throughout this whole period, and a study of his life mirrors many important developments in architecture, as well as having great intrinsic interest. In outlook and manner, though, Blomfield was quintessentially Edwardian, an archetypal representative of a fascinating era.

There has been a considerable increase in the number of publications dealing with late nineteenth- and early twentieth-century architecture recently, but this was not always the case. The writing of architectural history in the years following the Second World War was dominated by historians who sought to advance and consolidate the philosophy of the Modern Movement, which they wished to show as the inevitable outcome of historical, social and technological factors. Edwardian architects were considered only if their work could be seen to impinge upon this development. Voysey and Mackintosh for instance, became well known, but they were viewed from a single aspect and little was said of their contemporaries or the *milieu* in which they worked. Traditional architecture was largely ignored, despite the fact that some of its representatives were great architects by any standards, and that major parts of towns and cities were designed by those who did not form part of the modernist pedigree. The general disillusionment with modernism, though, has removed restrictions on a subject hitherto taboo. Written studies have dealt with architectural biography, the development of architectural history, architectural drawing and specific building types. In nearly all of these works Blomfield's name is prominent. This book seeks to describe the various aspects of Blomfield's involvement, and to present them within the context of his life.

The early part of Blomfield's career was dominated by his membership of the Norman Shaw circle. The Shaw 'family' was composed of young architects who were instrumental in the advancement of design in the 1880s. They were largely responsible for the founding of the Art Workers' Guild and the Arts and Crafts Exhibition Society, by which they attempted to raise the general standard of design. Blomfield thus came into contact with celebrated designers practising under the influence of William Morris. From the early 1890s, though, affected by both his personal taste and the researches that he had carried out for his books *The Formal Garden in England* (1892) and *A History of Renaissance Architecture in England, 1500–1800* (1897), he began to move away from arts and crafts affiliations. He interested himself in what he considered to be the true English tradition of restrained, unselfconscious and unpedantic classicism as practised by Wren and his contemporaries. He believed that a revival of this style would provide a sounder basis for architecture as it progressed into the twentieth century and had to provide for new large-scale buildings, often in important urban or rural locations. He used this style in his own designs, and was instrumental in establishing its prominence through his trenchant and scholarly writings. Although he was by no means the only exponent of classicism, it is due in no small part to Blomfield's efforts that it again became the dominant force in British architecture in the opening decades of this century.

The First World War brought about social changes which had far-reaching effects on architectural practice. Many of Blomfield's contemporaries faded from professional life, but despite advancing years he was able to adapt, accept new challenges and continue to work at full stretch, in terms of both practice and writing. His associations with professional bodies and committees, originally built up in the years before the war, were, if anything, expanded. An important member of the Royal Academy and the Royal Fine Art Commission, he was to the forefront in the great debates of the day, and was always ready to pronounce on a variety of matters concerned with questions of aesthetic merit, or to do battle in support of worthy causes such as the attempts to save Waterloo Bridge and Wren's City churches. Despite these crusading efforts he became a symbol of the architectural establishment, the epitome of reaction and conservatism, and his name was anathema to young architects. This, exemplified in his violent criticism of the Modern Movement, which reached its climax with the publication of his book *Modernismus* (1934), seems to have harmed his reputation for a generation. It is now time to reassess this important and influential architect.

CHAPTER 1
BEGINNINGS

Reginald Blomfield was a remarkable man, but he was also a member of a prolific and successful family which had produced a number of noteworthy offspring. He recognised this fact when, in 1916, he published his book *A Suffolk Family*. A substantial and well-presented history, it was nevertheless intended for private circulation and not as a rival to the erudite works on architecture that he had been writing for many years. Its production, though, emphasises the significance that he attached to his family background and indicates its relevance in developing an appreciation of Blomfield himself.

A Suffolk Family

The Blomfields, originally named Blomevil, came from Normandy at the time of the Conquest. They settled in East Anglia and held substantial lands in the Stowmarket and Ipswich areas. Here they flourished for many centuries as country gentlemen, merchants and farmers. Their continuity and importance is shown by the fact that in the early eighteenth century the seat of Four Elms in Stonham Parva was noted as having been the residence of one branch of the family for virtually six hundred years. Furthermore, between the end of the sixteenth century and the beginning of the eighteenth century, no fewer than fifteen Blomfields held the position of churchwarden in the parish of Stonham Aspal[1]. From the time of the Restoration, however, family fortunes began to decline. Wealth was dissipated into an increasing number of branches and offshoots and there was intermarriage with strict puritans whose attitudes were no longer in accord with the period. The decline and its effects were evident for over one hundred years, but by the beginning of the nineteenth century a revitalised line emerged which was to produce a number of talented and able people.

Reginald Blomfield was descended from two distinct parts of the family. His mother, Isabella, was one of the children of Charles James Blomfield, a distinguished clergyman, who was Bishop of London from 1828 to 1856. Her brothers, Frank and Arthur, were exceptional men of action and intelligence, who earned the nickname 'Thunder' and 'Lightning' during their undergraduate years at Cambridge. Frank was later drowned at sea whilst saving life, but Arthur went on to become a famous architect, the designer of churches and collegiate buildings, and the erstwhile employer of both the young Thomas Hardy and Reginald himself.[2]

Reginald Blomfield's father also came from a clerical background. George John Blomfield was the son of the Rector of Orsett in Essex. He, too, was ordained a priest in the Church of England, and held appointments at Bow in Devon (where Reginald was born in December 1856) and Dartford in Kent, before becoming Rector and Rural Dean of Aldington, Kent. Here, he built himself a new rectory and organised the restoration of the old church. Firmly established, he brought up a large brood of children, of whom he fathered eleven by his marriage to Isabella Blomfield.[3] Three of the children died in infancy, but of the remainder several went on to achieve success in later life.

The first son, Edward George, followed his father into the Anglican ministry, working at Portsea, and later at St Mark's Woolston, Southampton, where he was Vicar. He took his responsibilities so seriously that overwork may have contributed to his death at the early age of thirty-two in 1885. His brother, Charles James, became an army officer, demonstrating his prowess as a child by almost blinding the young Reginald with a shot from his catapult. He later served in the Middle East, South Africa and India, gaining awards for bravery and ending up with the rank of Major-General. He was also 'an amateur artist of unusual ability'.[4]

Reginald Theodore was the third son. He grew up in an atmosphere that must have been unusually competitive. His father was 'an able man, with a quick temper and a ready sense of humour, who loved a scrap'. In his *Memoirs*, however, Reginald states: 'I must have been a happy child with kind parents and relations, and a large family of brothers and sisters to fight and play with in that dear old Vicarage garden.'[5]

He was sent away to school at the age of eight in 1865 and his experiences at an academy in Brighton were far from happy. He later moved on to Haileybury College, and began a career which was, for the first few years, hardly sparkling. It is intimated in the *Memoirs* that at this time Reginald must have been a highly-strung, introverted and insecure youth. He established a collection of butterflies, kept pets and spent much of his time reading poetry, all solitary occupations.

Suddenly, however, from the age of sixteen, and after a severe reprimand from his father, who threatened him with a career as a post office clerk, he began to work hard and effectively, excelling in both physical and academic activities. He came out as head of both lower and upper fifth, moved directly into the upper sixth, and won several prizes. He also developed a taste for literature and the visual arts. This was not unusual, for Haileybury at that time possessed a remarkable collection of talented staff who were inspiring teachers.

Towards the end of his school career Reginald was entered for Oxford University, but in order to go there a scholarship was necessary, for his father was in a far from lucrative profession and Reginald was the third son. Following some worrying mishaps and a serious illness, he eventually gained a place at Exeter College, with sufficient income for a modest existence. It can be assumed that he enjoyed the intellectual and physical challenge and also the broadening of academic and artistic experience which the University afforded.

The *Memoirs* contain recollections of sporting occasions, with particular reference to rugby football and cricket at which he excelled, undergraduate horseplay, holidays on the river and academic activities. Blomfield worked hard at everything, so hard, in fact, that he virtually suffered a nervous breakdown when he was about to take 'Greats'. He was able to discipline himself just in time, however, and obtained a first-class degree. One of the examiners later wrote to him: 'Perhaps you have never realised what a brilliant little First Class that turned out to be: Conybeare, Jevons, Montague and yourself: what a Quartet! A Masterpiece!'[6]

Architectural Apprenticeship

Blomfield therefore left University with an excellent record of achievement, but with no clear idea as to the next stage of his career. He had a strong interest in the visual arts, but a private income was necessary to provide support for a potential painter or sculptor, and this was hardly forthcoming. The prospect of a humdrum, uncreative administrative future must have loomed before him. Fortunately, his uncle was by now a very successful architect and he generously allowed Reginald to become an articled pupil without the payment of the burdensome fees which were normally charged to aspiring professionals. However, despite a schoolboy enthusiasm for Piranesi and many hours spent in the Taylorian Museum copying the drawings of Raphael and Michelangelo, Blomfield was forced to admit that he 'came down from Oxford knowing nothing whatever about architecture.'[7] Yet his educational background was to provide a sound base for further development. The tough intellectual discipline of the classics, and an already apparent talent for drawing, enabled him to think clearly, concisely and in three dimensions. There is, though, none of the inevitability about his chosen career that is to be found in the case of his younger contemporary Edwin Lutyens, for instance. It seems likely that Blomfield would have made a success of any one of a number of professions.

He entered his uncle's practice in the autumn of 1881. Arthur W. Blomfield (1829–99) was Diocesan Architect to the See of Winchester and had charge of Salisbury, Canterbury, Lincoln and Chichester Cathedrals at various times. He not only designed many new churches, but was also involved with restoration work, some of which was perhaps extreme and over-zealous. Certain architectural critics have also found a hard and soulless quality in his original designs, although this is by no means always true. His practice started when the Gothic Revival was at its height and the style of many of his buildings bears witness to this, though he does not seem to have been a very committed Gothicist. Reginald Blomfield was out of sympathy with his uncle's architectural style, but found him 'a good draughtsman, a fine billiards player, a first-rate amateur actor, witty, humorous, and one of the most kindly and generous of men.'[8]

Others were not so charitable. Sir Edmund Beckett (1816–1905), later Lord Grimthorpe, a scourge of all architects and with whom Arthur Blomfield had several clashes, had a very low opinion of him: 'He is a blockhead in every way', he complained. 'I have always thought him a very feeble creature with nothing of his father [Bishop Blomfield] except his ill-temper and intolerance.'[9]

Reginald's first reaction to office work was one of disappointment. He had expected a keen intellectual and artistic atmosphere, where creative development was paramount and where aesthetic problems were deeply discussed. Instead, he found a small professional practice run by conventional people. The other pupils did not show an overwhelming enthusiasm for architecture. They were more interested in discussing sport and salacious news reports in the popular press. Blomfield did not allow this atmosphere to divert him. He reacted by working diligently even though his serious outlook and arrogant intellectual stance may have made him unpopular from time to time, perhaps even an object of ridicule, and he was involved in one or two 'scraps' in the office.

Arthur Blomfield himself did the designing and the younger men were only concerned with the most menial tasks such as finishing drawings or producing the multitudinous copies which were required for contract purposes. For the indolent, this work resulted only in the acquisition of mechanical skills. For someone like Blomfield, though, used to intellectual discipline and full of curiosity and the will to learn, much could be gained by studying the work of others.

Probably the most stimulating project to appear in the office during his time was a scheme not initiated by his uncle but by George Edmund Street (1824–81), one of the most influential and talented architects of the Gothic Revival, who had died during the construction of his greatest secular building, the Royal Courts of Justice in the Strand. The job was bequeathed to Arthur Blomfield, who had to cope with the completion of the construction and detail design. The scale of this work was such that it was bound to involve everyone in the office in a great variety of activity. Reginald had the laborious and finicky job of scaling down the plans, but, more rewardingly, he was also occupied on site where he could see detail and decorative work going ahead, in particular some modelled panels in the interior for which he had special responsibility.

The value of this to the aspiring architect could not be overestimated, but it was generally felt in professional circles that rather more academic stimulus was required if the pupil was to develop confidence in his own attitudes and approaches. To this end, young men were sent to the Royal Academy School, which they attended two or three evenings each week. Reginald Blomfield enrolled in 1882 and worked under the direction of the Master, Richard Phené Spiers (1838–1916). Spiers had been educated in the French Beaux-Arts system, the lengthy and formal academic education which relied upon the mastery of classical design through extensive study of worthy precedents. This was, of course, part of the French academic tradition, and nothing like it existed in Britain, either in form or content. Doubtless Spiers brought this experience to bear in his teaching, and Blomfield considered that he was 'of real service to all of us who were really keen on our work'.[10]

Apart from Spiers there were a number of 'visitors' to the Royal Academy School. These were experienced architects who would provide criticism and advice to students about the project-work that was set at the school. They were well-known and proficient men – Bodley, Pearson, Waterhouse and Street – but their value as teachers seems to have been rather doubtful. In his *Memoirs*, Blomfield will not admit to their having had any effect upon him, and their 'visits' were probably of a rather superficial kind. It is also possible that the young men were out of sympathy with the Gothic Revival to which most of the 'visitors' seem to have been committed. Significantly, Blomfield only mentions Richard Norman Shaw as an influence. Shaw was a kindly and conscientious man, but he was also the leading exponent of the foremost architectural style of the day, and he demonstrated a flexibility in his approach to design that allowed it to develop, instead of remaining bogged down in an outmoded philosophy. He was, therefore, undoubtedly more attractive to the students.

Blomfield prospered at the Royal Academy School, and his academic and artistic talent helped him to rise above his contemporaries. He received the prize for the Junior School in 1882, and in the following year was awarded the Senior School prize for the design of a London street house. In this scheme he arranged the accommodation on four main floors, the overall planning being similar to that developed for other buildings of the type which were in vogue at the time and whose chief exponents were Shaw and Ernest George. A report on Blomfield's project notes that 'the style is a free treatment of the English Renaissance,'[11] a phrase commonly used in architectural journalism and sufficiently vague to cover a multitude of sins. In fact, the design, with its gable, pinnacles, grotesque beasts and decorative panels illustrating the seasons of the year, is clearly derived from fashionable contemporary work. The arcading to the ground and first floors, more particularly, reminds one of Shaw's work at 196, Queensgate, Kensington or Albert Hall Mansions. The overall effect of the design is somewhat stilted, despite the use of every decorative device that could be mustered. By the time Blomfield wrote his *Memoirs*, some fifty years later, he was embarrassed by this ornate and picturesque scheme. 'It was a wretched affair, but I suppose the others were worse', he wrote.[12]

In the autumn of 1883 he completed his training, Spiers writing to his father

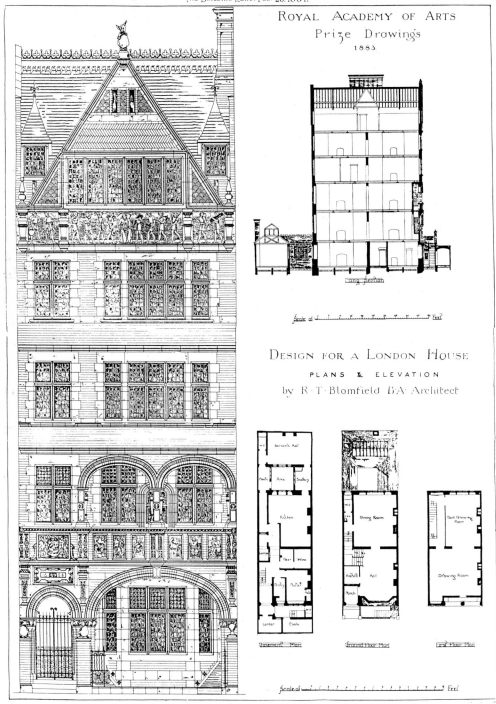

THE BUILDING NEWS, FEB. 29.1884.

ROYAL ACADEMY OF ARTS
Prize Drawings
1883

DESIGN FOR A LONDON HOUSE

PLANS & ELEVATION

by R·T·Blomfield B·A· Architect

1 The Royal Academy Senior School Prize Drawing, 1883

on 19 January 1884 that his son's progress in the school had been 'most gratify-ing' and trusting that his son's practical career would be 'as brilliant as his student's career.'[13] At this stage, also, he made the decision to leave his uncle's office. There was some sort of disagreement between the two temperamental men which precipitated the move, but one suspects that the time was right for the younger Blomfield to make the break: he had acquired a degree of practical knowledge and self-confidence, and possibly felt inhibited by the office itself and the type of design work that was produced. As an ambitious person he would wish to make his own way, and control his own career to as great an extent as possible.

He did not begin in practice straight away, but resolved upon a period of recreation and study. To this end he undertook a four-month tour of France and Spain. Having set out with a companion, he eventually branched out independently and travelled around in solitary and often uncomfortable fashion, sketching and recording avidly as he went. He confined his drawings mainly to details of sculpture, carving and architectural ornament, and the buildings that he sketched were nearly always Gothic or Romanesque. The choice of subject matter was typical of the period. Eclectic architecture relied upon the designer having a catalogue of quaint architectural features in his head. Travel and sketching was the ideal way to build up such a compendium. Later on in his career Blomfield was critical of this approach, but at the time produced about one hundred drawings and there seems to have been a rapid development in his technical competence as a draughtsman.[14]

Blomfield tells us in the *Memoirs* that upon his return to England he decided to write a history of Romanesque architecture. The massive qualities of struc-ture in that style greatly appealed to him, as opposed to those inherent in Gothic design. His project, though, was over-ambitious. It is unlikely that even he could have carried out such a taxing work so early in his career. Instead, he was persuaded by his father to narrow his scope drastically and he settled on the topic of old Sussex ironwork which formed the basis of an article published in the magazine *The Portfolio*. Such studies were fairly com-mon at the time, and architects were increasingly using features taken from the vernacular. Norman Shaw, for instance, in his extensions to the painter J. C. Horsley's house at Willesley, Kent, had 'bell pulls, casement fasteners and gas brackets . . . all fashioned in the manner of old wealden ironwork.'[15]

The consequences of undertaking the study were to have far-reaching effects upon Blomfield's career, for the project represents an early instance of the type of reseach and writing that he was to produce for most of his working life, though often on a much grander scale, and in parallel with archi-tectural practice.

Early Practice

The practice that Blomfield built up, however, had humble beginnings. It was expected that any young architect making his own way should be prepared to accept poverty and disappointment for at least the first three or four years. There was much to learn of practical matters that only experience could teach and up to the start of his own practice it is doubtful whether he had ever been responsible for a complete building. He began in 1884, but commissions were very slow to arrive at his office at 17, Southampton Street, WC2, and he had to wait for 'such work as came [his] way.'[16] In a list of works compiled after his death, there are no buildings at all shown before 1886. This particular year, however, seems to have signalled an improvement in Blomfield's fortunes, for although he had become engaged to Frances Mary Burra, the daughter of a Sussex landowner, some three years earlier, it was not until 1886 that he felt that he could afford to marry. Indeed, prior to this, financial stringency was such tht he had even to give up cricket, which involved expensive social commitments, and to substitute lawn tennis as an outlet for his sporting and physical energies.

Some initial contacts for commissions were made through personal acquaintances and although his immediate family were not rich, there appear to have been some wealthier relatives at least one of whom employed him. His wife, moreover, was a member of a family which owned estates just to the north of Rye, in Sussex. His uncle, after the 'misunderstanding' between them had been patched up, recommended him for one or two jobs, perhaps resulting from his important connections with the hierarchy of the Church of England, and he also started work at his old school, Haileybury, in Hertfordshire. Inevitably, though, most of the commissions in the early years were small in scale, but it is possible to detect a pattern that is reflected in the building types he designed up to the outbreak of the First World War: educational institutions, domestic work, church restoration, and a small number of public buildings. Some of this work would have been familiar to Blomfield from his uncle's practice, but, to a considerable extent, he must have relied upon personal experience to increase his knowledge and confidence.

Blomfield's early projects do not display great originality, neither is there much evidence of any personal stamp. Some are attractive, but others may seem a little clumsy or rigid in design. In the main, though, they are derivative, and not very different from the kind of work produced by any number of competent architects of the day. Increasingly, there is evidence of arts and crafts influence, particularly in decoration. During the first few years of practice Blomfield was really feeling his way aesthetically and coming to terms with the technical and financial constraints that help to shape buildings and occupy much of the architect's attention.

The first building of any substance that he was called upon to design was

2 Bradby Hall, Haileybury, shortly after completion

for his old school, where his uncle had already been architecturally active. A hall was to be constructed in memory of Dr Bradby, one of Haileybury's foremost teachers, who had helped to shape the philosophy of the school in the early days after its refounding in the 1850s. He had been headmaster during Blomfield's time there, and was gratefully remembered by his former pupil.

The Bradby Memorial Hall is of the tall, gabled type popular for school buildings in the 1880s. The main internal space is at first-floor level, with smaller rooms below. It has a high roof with exposed beams, supported on a timber framework which drops down to enclose and support a gallery, running round the main body of the hall. It is lit by a great arched window in the gable end and by the gallery windows which project externally through the line of the roof slope.

Structure and form are cleverly integrated, and Blomfield also seems to have given much attention to the detail design of the building, particularly the panelling and the joinery to the interior of the hall. The overall appearance of the building reflects early seventeenth-century work, and perhaps the well-worn phrase 'a free treatment of the English Renaissance' could be used to describe it. The lantern and cupola high up on the roof and the decorative wall panels are typical of the style.

3 Blomfield's perspective drawing of the interior of Bradby Hall, 1887

4 Design for the cover to Hunt's catalogue of rainwater heads

It is a design that despite its good points fails in consistency, as might be expected from a first major commission. It is overwrought and insufficiently single-minded or direct in intent. It also fails to respond to the rather austere and restrained character of Haileybury engendered by William Wilkins many years earlier.

The building contractor for the Bradby Hall was John Alfred Hunt of Hoddesdon. Hunt, some eight years senior to Blomfield, seems to have developed a reputable business. The involvement of the two men in the construction of the hall appears to have led to a long-lasting relationship which must have been of benefit to both parties. For instance, in 1887, we find Blomfield designing a 'catalogue of wrought and cast lead [rainwater] heads' for Hunt, to be made at his Hoddesdon works. Blomfield went to some lengths with the title page for the catalogue, which is drawn in an interesting arts and crafts style. In the same year, he designed at least four houses for the St Catharine's Estate, Broxbourne, Hertfordshire, which Hunt was developing at the time. The estate was to consist of substantial, upper-middle-class houses, for lease, which in spite of their pleasant semi-rural position would be within easy commuting distance of London. They were 'all carefully designed by eminent Architects . . . and built and finished by the Messrs Hunt in the best substantial manner.'[17] Blomfield's work here is respectable rather than outstanding. The houses are not much different in style to their neighbours, solid, big-boned villas with the typical stock in trade of 'Olde English': gables, tile-hanging and half-timbering, so popular in domestic work in the last few decades of

5 Two of the houses for the St Catherine's estate, Broxbourne

6 The Public Library and Art School, Hertford

7 Beckley Church, nr Rye, Sussex

the nineteenth century. One house, however, was described as being 'artistically planned in the Georgian style by Mr. Reginald T. Blomfield, MA', fore-
shadowing the move towards classicism later in his career.

In the late 1880s Blomfield received two commissions in Hertford, and by
this time he must have been fairly well known in the locality, despite the fact
that his office was in Bloomsbury. They were a covered market hall and a
public library, both designed in conjunction with W. H. Wilds, a local architect. The market hall was a basic utilitarian structure, but the library, which
also accommodated an art school at first-floor level, was a half-timbered,
gabled building, its architectural vocabulary not unlike that of the houses
in Broxbourne. Blomfield did not seem particularly happy working in this
style, and the building has a rather stiff feeling about it, not normally associated
with the picturesque and romantic character to which it aspires. Perhaps his
use of these elements did not carry much conviction. It was a style that he
was soon to forsake.

Neither did he feel at home in Gothic, yet a significant proportion of his
work in the 1880s was ecclesiastical, and concerned with the restoration of
medieval buildings. He was not dogmatic about restoration and whilst eschew-
ing the drastic measures of the High Victorian Gothicists he was not wholly
in accord with the approach of Morris's Society for the Protection of Ancient
Buildings.

His work is generally sensitive and responds to the character of the building.

8 Blomfield's perspective drawing of the rehabilitated Brooklands, 1890

Examples are to be found at Boxford Church, Suffolk (1886), Warnham Church, Sussex (1886), St George, Ivychurch, Kent (1888) and Beckley Church, near Rye, Sussex (1888). The latter is located in an area where Frances Blomfield's family was influential, and he undertook restoration and additions here up to 1925.

The figure of J. A. Hunt appears again towards the end of the 1880s, this time as a general contractor for one of Blomfield's most significant early projects, the renovation of a large house at Weybridge, Surrey, known as Brooklands. During the first part of his career, Blomfield worked extensively on domestic restorations and this was the first of any size. Brooklands was owned by his cousin, Arthur Brook, and was originally built in about 1860 without the employment of an architect. Eventually the roof began to slip, and in 1889 Reginald Blomfield was brought in to effect repairs, alterations and additions. The 'Specification of Works' refers to the 'New roof, Chimneys, Attic floor and Staircase . . . new roof to the N.E. and W. Wings and to the Clock Tower and all repairs to existing fabric.'

Blomfield tackled the work, both internally and externally, with gusto, and there are features typical of his contemporary style, heavily influenced by Shaw. The building must have been rather gaunt originally, and although Blomfield added to the height he probably made it a jollier place. There are tall chimneys, some capped by arts and crafts canopies, finials to the ridge line, a prodigious number of gables, dormers and roof lanterns. The outline

9 A photograph of the tradesmen engaged in the works at 'Brooklands'

of the building is exciting, if disorganised, and the elevation to the entrance court presents a jumble of windows of all shapes and sizes, reflecting, most likely, an internal struggle brought about by the reorganisation of the accommodation. There is evidence elsewhere of attempts at control, and a determination to regularise the fenestration, as on the garden front, but this cannot have been an easy project to organise and execute. The low addition to one side of the house is more in keeping with Blomfield's later work and is dignified and urbane.

If the house has Shavian overtones externally, then the evidence of Shaw's influence is more than borne out by the interiors, especially the billiards room, with its fireplace recess, lit from the side and fitted with seats; the arched opening leading to a raised platform in the bay window at the end of the room, and the sumptuous detailing reminiscent of late seventeenth-century English country-house work. Then there is the staircase with its newels and electrolier. Blomfield seems to have enjoyed designing every detail of this building, and perhaps he saw it as a great opportunity to put into practice some of the principles of the Arts and Crafts movement to which, at this time, he was committed.

Finally, mention must be made of the town house at 20, James Street, Buckingham Gate, Westminster, which shows Blomfield using the 'free Renaissance' with confidence, aplomb and, apparently, enjoyment. The overall effect is whimsical, but all the elements have been confidently handled. The size and form of the building are very similar to the student scheme of some four years earlier, but a greater degree of relaxation and maturity is evident. There is a tall, stepped gable, typical of the period, oriel window, modelled frieze and other picturesque details. The whole thing is an imaginative mixture of imprecisely definable seventeenth- and eighteenth-century stylistic elements, but the results of scholarship are also in evidence. *The Builder* notes that 'the pointing is a little unusual, a flat, slightly recessed strip between the bricks, lined in the centre with a hollow of semi-circular section; it was revived by Mr. Blomfield from a form used about 150 years ago.'[18]

This is, undoubtedly, the most charming of the early works, but shows Blomfield coming to grips with historic precedent which affects the detail, as well as the general theme.

Arts and Crafts Involvements

The most outstanding influence in this early work, it will have been noted, is that of Richard Norman Shaw (1831–1912), one of the few contemporary architects genuinely admired by Blomfield. By a lucky coincidence Blomfield was introduced to the Shaw circle early in his career. Blomfield's practice

10 Blomfield's drawing of the billiards room, 'Brooklands', 1889

SKETCHES OF LONDON STREET ARCHITECTURE, III.—No. 20, JAMES-STREET, BUCKINGHAM GATE.
MR. REGINALD BLANFIELD, ARCHITECT.

11 20 James Street, Buckingham Gate. A drawing by W. Curtis Green

was based on the second floor of No. 17, Southampton Street, Bloomsbury. The office on the floor below was also occupied by an architect, Edward Prior (1852–1932), some four years older than Blomfield. The two men had much in common: both were sportsmen, both were keen thinkers who held strong personal views, and both were outspoken in their opinions. Their meeting and subsequent friendship were particularly advantageous for Blomfield, as Prior, an ex-pupil of Richard Norman Shaw, was one of the illustrious Shaw 'family', and Prior drew his new friend into the group.[19]

This 'family' was composed of the pupils, ex-pupils and employees of Shaw. There were no rules of membership, it was simply an informal group. When Blomfield was introduced, the most prominent members were, besides Prior, Mervyn Macartney (1853–1932), Ernest Newton (1856–1922), and Gerald

Horsley (1862–1917), who were pupils and assistants, and William Richard Lethaby (1857–1931), Shaw's chief draughtsman. All became important architects in the post-Shaw generation, and although Norman Shaw himself was not an intellectual, he seemed to attract some of the best creative talents and minds.

It was mainly through the efforts of the 'family', for instance, that the Art Workers' Guild was founded. This was established in 1884, but grew out of the St George's Art Society which Shaw's pupils had set up some years before. Macartney and Horsley were the Guild's first secretaries and, by 1885, Blomfield had begun to attend Guild events, joining officially in 1887. Its aims, in Blomfield's opinion, were to 'bring all the arts together, to place artists and craftsmen of all sorts in touch with one another, without any foolish attempt to discriminate between fine art and any other art. It was an honest and sincere attempt to find a common standpoint from which all the graphic and plastic arts and crafts should be approached.'[20]

The Guild, which had premises in Bloomsbury, was really a kind of social club for arts and crafts artists, architects and craftsmen. There were formal evening meetings which were devoted to particular topics or demonstrations of crafts, and there were also informal gatherings and discussions. Blomfield thus had the opportunity to meet people from all branches of the arts, but the Guild was especially popular with architects. By 1889 the membership included not only the bright young men of the 'family', but other outstanding young architects, such as C. F. A. Voysey and Halsey Ricardo, and distinguished men of the older generation, including practitioners as diverse as Basil Champneys, John Belcher, T. G. Jackson and J. F. Bentley.

Blomfield eventually became Honorary Secretary of the Guild. Quite often members would dine at his house, 39, Woburn Square, before their meetings, and fellow-members such as Cobden Sanderson, the bookbinder, and Charles Furse, the painter, became clients. He was pleased, too, to make the acquaintance of the legendary William Morris, whose poetic work he had admired as a schoolboy. He saw a great deal of Morris in 1892 when he was Secretary of the Guild and Morris was President, and, although he had no time for 'Art Socialism', Blomfield wrote:

> All that I saw and knew of him deepened my admiration for this
> splendid man. He asked me down to Hammersmith, where he showed
> me his books and talked to me in his garden, easily, naturally and
> without any pomp and ceremony, and I came away feeling that my
> boyish admiration for the author of *The Earthly Paradise* had not been
> misplaced.[21]

Oddly, Norman Shaw, mentor of many of the Guild's architect members, thought little of Morris, and considered that his socialism 'was just a pose', and that Morris himself was simply a 'tradesman, whose only object was to make money'.[22]

The Guild, therefore, contained an array of talented but diverse individuals, several of whom became involved in other projects allied to the arts and crafts aims, one of the most important of which was the establishment of the Arts and Crafts Exhibition Society, founded in 1888. Blomfield records:

> A strong committee was formed; Walter Crane was President, and the Committee included Morris, Burne-Jones, J. D. Sedding, the architect; Harry Bates, the sculptor; De Morgan, who wrote novels and painted china and pottery; Cobden Sanderson, the bookbinder; and behind them were the serried ranks of the Art Workers' Guild, including a group of young architects, impatient to break through the trade ring of furnishers, upholsterers and decorators, and emancipate the individual artist and the actual designer.[23]

The philosophy of the Society was to remove barriers between artists and craftsmen. It was not merely a discussion forum, but existed in order to publicise the work of members, thereby spreading its aims. Apart from the exhibitions themselves, a catalogue was published in which members sometimes presented short essays. For the 1889 exhibition, for instance, Blomfield wrote on 'Book Illustration and Decoration', in which he followed closely 'the teaching of Morris in regard to typography and the printed page.'[24]

He later lectured, wrote essays and produced design work for the exhibitions, including the wrought-iron gates displayed in 1896, which were subsequently taken by Norman Shaw for use at New Scotland Yard.[25]

Events were held somewhat irregularly, and, after the first two years, not on an annual basis. Blomfield was involved with the staging of the exhibitions:

12 Park entrance gates displayed at the Arts and Crafts Exhibition, 1896

29

'I recall long days of work with him [Mervyn Macartney] in the nineties in the New Gallery', he wrote, 'selecting and arranging works for the Arts and Crafts Exhibitions.'[26]

It may seem strange in the light of his subsequent attitudes that Blomfield was so closely involved with the Arts and Crafts movement, even in the early days of his career, yet he always believed in comprehensivenes of design and felt that the architect should have control over the whole range of work, in order to produce a satisfying unity of intent and appearance. He did not believe, however, that he should be able to exercise the crafts under his control. In the case of furniture design, for instance, his opinion was that the architect should have 'sufficient knowledge of the crafts to settle for the craftsmen the all-important points of scale and proportion to the rest of the design'.[27]

This is further emphasised by another venture stemming from his involvement with the Arts and Crafts movement, the founding of Kenton & Co. Indeed, the firm to some extent directly owed its existence to the activities of the Arts and Crafts Exhibition Society. Blomfield and Macartney were two of the members who where deputed to find good examples of contemporary furniture for exhibitions, by visiting principal London shops. The results of the shopping expeditions were so disappointing and the furniture so uninspiring that 'with Lethaby, as usual our fount of inspiration, we decided to make ourselves into a firm of furniture designers and makers.'[28]

The principal members of the firm, which was set up in 1890, were Blomfield, Macartney, Lethaby, Ernest Gimson (1864–1919), Sidney Barnsley (1863–1926) and a retired cavalry officer, Colonel Mallet, who took no active part in design but had an administrative rôle. In addition, Stephen Webb, a draughtsman and designer, was associated with Kenton and Co. for a short time. Each member subscribed a sum of money for the purchase of materials. They also employed 'four or five of the best workmen [they] could get' and in their premises, over stables at the back of Bedford Row, designs were produced which were often simple in concept, but usually elegant, of sophisticated form and quite lavish in the use of woods and veneers. Among other things, Blomfield designed a rosewood settee, the arms of which had to be modelled in clay before wood-working could begin. Another design had a border with an inlay of rabbits eating lettuce, an example of the sort of charming arts and crafts motif he was soon to forsake.

After a year of production there was an exhibition and a large quantity of furniture was sold. This was encouraging, but the profit was minimal, and it was eventually decided that in order to make money more capital had to be injected into the firm. The participants were thus encouraged to think more closely about whether they wished to devote themselves to furniture manufacture or to give more time to their main careers. As it happened, all except Gimson and Barnsley wished to give up furniture production, and so, after a short life, the firm was wound up in 1892.

13 Design for a sideboard for W. Alexander, 1893

14 Rosewood and cane settee made by Kenton & Co.

Blomfield says: 'Lethaby, Macartney and I decided to cut our loss and concentrate on the practice of architecture.' An expansion of Kenton would have required full-time involvement and, he continues, 'Macartney's practice and mine were steadily growing and required all our energies. Moreover . . . I was already engaged on a considerable undertaking, a history of Renaissance Architecture in England.'[29]

That Blomfield should choose to devote time to historical and literary endeavour is indicative of his changing priorities. Indeed, it is by this work, perhaps more than his buildings, that he is remembered today. He began writing on architectural topics at the start of his career, and it is something that he was drawn to throughout the whole of his active life.

CHAPTER 2
TWO BOOKS

Most architects find it difficult to express themselves in words, especially when it comes to making clear and unpretentious statements about design. Blomfield was certainly an exception to this rule, and he is as notable for his written work as he is for his buildings. Indeed, some may find more refinement of style and clarity of intent in the Blomfield of the printed page than in the man of bricks and mortar.

The foundations for his literary career were established by two influential books, written in the 1890s, which had been preceded by a series of earlier studies.

Early Writings

The slow start to Blomfield's practice meant that he often found himself with spare time. He used this profitably, for, as he tells us in the *Memoirs*: 'In the intervals [in practice] I drew and measured old buildings.'[1] He had been doing this since his student days and recalled that 'about the year 1882–83 . . . I was rambling about the Weald of Kent on a "penny farthing" bicycle, 56 in. high, in pursuit of 17th-century domestic architecture.'[2] This type of study was not only intrinsically interesting, but provided a resource which helped to expand the vocabulary of forms for use in design. It also enabled him to develop a firm base for future studies in architectural history.

His earliest study, 'Old Sussex Ironwork', which he began on his return from the Continent in 1884, formed the basis for an article on 'Sussex Foundries' published in *The Portfolio*, 'an excellent monthly magazine edited by Philip Hamerton'. This was followed in 1887 and 1888 by further articles, the appearance of which encouraged Blomfield to persevere with his critical and historical studies. *The Portfolio* was a magazine of the arts. It was well printed and set out, with plentiful sketches and illustrations, although rather self-conscious in its style of presentation. It seems to have been favoured by young and progressive artists. The inclusion of Blomfield's work must have helped to make his name familiar to a discerning, if limited, public. His facility in sketching and the charming nature of his drawings were probably important factors in the acceptance of his work, and in some cases he provided illustrations for the writings of other authors.

Three separate articles, with the overall title 'Half Timbered Houses in the Weald of Kent and Neighbourhood, by R.T. Blomfield, M.A.', were published in 1887. They were written in a readable style and a broad view was taken of the topic, with notes covering aspects of construction and details of social history. There were comments on current design issues, something that

15 Blomfield's drawing of Knole, Kent. One of the buildings illustrated in 'Some Architects of the English Renaissance'

16 The Triangular Lodge, Rushton, mentioned in 'Some Architects of the English Renaissance'

is evident in many of his later writings. He also mentioned the lack of a scholarly history of English art, and it may be that his own work on English Renaissance architecture, to be published some ten years later, was already in his mind. Certainly, most subsequent articles were concerned with some aspect of this subject. For instance, 'Some Architects of the English Renaissance 1550–1650' appeared in 1888, again in three instalments.

The following year saw his publication of work on Inigo Jones, well supported by some of Jones's own drawings. This was followed up, in 1890, by the record of a walking tour in the West Country with Edward Prior and Ernest Newton. It does not contain any details of Blomfield's lively arguments with Prior, but confines itself to sketches of buildings, such as Montacute House, with descriptive and historical notes. Blomfield's clear narrative style leads the reader pleasantly through the material. Incidental details picturesquely evoking the English countryside are included ('Pigs grub about under the apple trees'). The whole captures the romantic atmosphere, as though the ambience of the architecture demands as much attention as scholarly description.

These articles for *The Portfolio* demonstrate Blomfield's developing technique.[3] Later, much of the material on particular architects was incorporated into the two books which Blomfield wrote in the 1890s and which were a direct consequence of earlier publications. *The Formal Garden in England* and *A History of Renaissance Architecture in England, 1500–1800* were published in 1892 and 1897 respectively. These books made Blomfield's name known to a wide public and, more important in terms of his practice, to potential clients. They also established him firmly as an important architectural writer. The timing of their appearance was opportune. Blomfield seems to have had the happy knack throughout his career of producing the right work at the right moment, and neatly filling gaps in existing literature.

'The Formal Garden in England'

Blomfield's first book was published at a time when there were two apparently conflicting theories of garden design; it helped to promote one of these views and, in doing so, criticised the other. This brought about a confrontation which, although unpleasant, eventually led to the reconciliation of the two philosophies and the development of a new English tradition.

It is interesting to look briefly at the background against which the book was written, so that its impact can be understood. The mid nineteenth century had seen a degeneration in the art of garden design. There existed a rather stilted Italianate formalism, usually adopted by architects working in the classical tradition, and also the whimsical 'Gardenesque', full of twists and turns and hidden nooks stuffed with ornaments, but with little design 'backbone'. In addition, there was a craze for 'bedding out' in which plants were raised in the controlled conditions made possible by the development of the hot house, and then set out in the garden in their hundreds in banal geometrical patterns. This trend was vigorously opposed by one of the most influential and best known garden designers of the nineteenth century, William Robinson. In *The English Flower Garden* of 1883, Robinson complained that 'the beautiful forms of flowers are degraded to the level of crude colour to make a design and without reference to the form of beauty of the plants'.[4] The whole was no more interesting than an oilcloth pattern.

Robinson was therefore opposed to sterile formalism and contrived whimsicality, and he pursued what he considered to be a more 'natural' type of design from the 1860s onwards. He was well established by the time Blomfield came on the scene and had spread his influence through his periodicals and, later, the work of his distinguished disciple, Gertrude Jekyll. Yet, at the same time, a different style had begun to flourish, which came to fruition in the 1870s with the emergence of the so-called 'Queen Anne' revival. 'Old-fashioned' gardens were preferred, modelled on seventeenth- and early eighteenth-century examples, in many cases, or deriving their inspiration from even earlier periods. Modesty and simplicity were important. Ideally, they were enclosed by walls and there were paths, ponds, bowers, arbours, summer houses, sundials and sculptural incidents, all related by an uncomplicated geometry. Topiary was much in evidence and humble plants such as sunflowers, hollyhocks, and columbine abounded. The origin of these 'old-fashioned' gardens dates back to the mid nineteenth century when interest was initially stirred by the Pre-Raphaelites and the Morris circle among others. They appealed greatly to the liberal middle classes in the 1880s and 1890s. Not only were their philosophical and associational overtones right, but the form and scale of such gardens were eminently suitable for suburban villas.[5]

17 'The Old Gardens at Brickwall'.
A drawing by F. Inigo Thomas
from *The Formal Garden in England*

THE OLD GARDENS AT BRICKWALL NEAR NORTHIAM : SUSSEX

Blomfield, as might be expected from his arts and crafts background, favoured the 'old-fashioned' garden. His personal bias towards restraint, strong design control and intellectual and aesthetic honesty led him in this direction also. He felt that there should be no attempt at pseudo-naturalism but a frank admission that a garden was, by its very nature, artificial. Both house and garden were man-made and their design should be controlled and complementary. This control, moreover, should come from the architect.

The Formal Garden in England sets out this case. It cannot really be said, though, as Blomfield claims in Chapter IV, that, 'until quite recently little attention has been paid to the formal garden', as the subject was quite often discussed at meetings of the Art Workers' Guild.[6] J. D. Sedding, the architect, a member of the Guild, published a book on the same subject just before Blomfield's came out, entitled *Garden Craft Old and New*. It appeared in 1891, shortly before its author's death. Although Sedding supported Blomfield's views, he recollected 'feeling a little annoyed that, though I saw him every fortnight at the Guild, he had never said a word to me about it, and had stolen a march on me, though he knew that I had been working for some time on this subject.'[7]

Nevertheless, although Sedding's book did not achieve the popularity of Blomfield's, both works incurred the wrath of Robinson, who saw himself, perhaps, as the one true prophet of modern garden design. He resented interlopers, particularly architects, whose intervention he regarded as disastrous, basing his views on the work of such men as Barry. He railed against these 'broken brick' gardeners, and talked of the 'frivolities of paper plans' probably without really understanding the nature of the new opposition. His specific reply to Sedding and Blomfield was *Garden Design and Architects' Gardens*. This response was, in Blomfield's view, 'violent'. Sedding was in no position to continue the argument, of course, but Blomfield, unable to resist a 'good scrap', pointed out in the preface to the second edition of *The Formal Garden* that 'Mr. Robinson's irritation had betrayed him into unnecessary blunders as well as gratuitous discourtesy!' It was, says Blomfield, 'altogether a pretty little controversy.'[8]

Robinson was, perhaps, unwise to become entangled with so fluent and competent a writer as Blomfield, whose facility with argument and ideas contributed to the success of his book, which ran into new editions even after the turn of the century. Ostensibly, the book makes a case for the formal garden and surveys the development of the English garden in the sixteenth, seventeenth and eighteenth centuries. It provides rich and varied examples of the gardens themselves and their components and notes the principles upon which they were designed. Underlying the whole work, however, are Blomfield's ideas about the scope of the architect's activity and the need in design for 'the finer scholarship which loves the past and holds thereby the key to its meaning.'[9]

SUNDIAL IN A SCOTCH GARDEN

18 'Sundial in a Scotch Garden'. A drawing by Thomas from *The Formal Garden*

Throughout the book can be seen the chief characteristics of Blomfield's literary manner: concise and perceptive historical comment; the adoption of a theoretical stance and its support by the use of examples; the denigration of opposite viewpoints, also with the support of examples; sound common sense and practicality; wit and sarcasm; an interest in personalities and a broad streak of romanticism. Taken together, these are lively, informative and thought-provoking and explain the author's consistent success with written work.

The book opens with an attack on the landscape gardener, who comes in for scathing criticism throughout:

The question at issue is a very simple one. Is the garden to be considered in relation to the house, and as an integral part of a design

19 'Garden Gate, Avebury, Wiltshire'. A drawing by Thomas from *The Formal Garden*

which depends for its success on the combined effect of the house and garden; or is the house to be ignored in dealing with the garden? The latter is the position of the landscape gardener in real fact.[10]

Apart from this initial chapter, setting out the argument, the rest of the book falls into two main sections with a conclusion. The first is a survey of the development of the formal garden design in England, referring particularly to the works of writers such as Thomas Hill, Gervase Markham and William Lawson; some pre eighteenth-century gardens are described. Then follow chapters dealing with the elements of formal garden design, ranging from fishponds to dovecotes, from parterres to palisades and from gatehouses to sundials. These are illustrated with charming and apposite pen-and-ink drawings by the architect, F. Inigo Thomas, whose work does much to complement and enhance Blomfield's text, and with contemporary engravings. Although taken from historical examples these illustrations form a catalogue of value to anyone wishing to construct a new formal garden. They are certainly sufficient to whet the architectural appetite of a potential client. The book then concludes with more attacks on the insensitivities of the landscape gardener.

Throughout, Blomfield pleads for formal design but in the most romantic terms. Although it is a persuasive way of writing it does underline Blomfield's contemporary attitude, a nostalgic hankering after an era when there existed 'a tradition of good taste'. He describes a garden in a sleepy country town which might survive from these days, and in which there were, 'old-fashioned flowers against the red-brick wall and a broad stretch of velvety turf set off by ample paths of gravel, and at one corner, perhaps, a dainty summer-house of brick with marble floor and panelled sides; and all so quiet and sober'.[11] Along with this romanticism, there is a related awareness of national identity and the belief that national characteristics are an important influence on

20 A view of Point Hill from the precipitous garden

design. This theme is emphasised more and more in Blomfield's work as the years pass, but it is noticeable even in the *Formal Garden*: 'The best English tradition has always been on the side of refinement and reserve; it has loved beauty – not the obvious beauty of the south, but the charm and tenderness, the inexpressible sweetness of faces, that fill the memory like half-remembered music'.[12]

This sort of writing could well become cloying but it is merely one ingredient of Blomfield's rich mix. Sarcasm is never far away: 'Kent was followed by 'Capability' Brown, who began as a kitchen gardener, but he took the judicious line that knowledge hampered originality. He accordingly dispensed with any training in design, and rapidly rose to eminence.'[13] There is also citing of amusing, yet learned, curiosities, such as Didymus Mountaine's advice, culled from Philostratus, that in order to protect a garden against hail, 'you drag a Marsh tortoise' round the garden on its back, and then place it still on its back on a little mound, carefully banking it up, so that the tortoise cannot tumble over or do anything but flap its legs. This is supposed to frighten away the hail.'[14]

Overall, then, the little book combined many successful ingredients. The enthusiasm with which it was written commended its author to the owners of such gardens. It also helped to encourage the revival of formal garden design, as Blomfield's career testifies. Gradually, though, the 'formal' and the 'natural' merged, as is evident in the work of Gertrude Jekyll who, partly through her association with Edwin Lutyens, forged the styles together.

Harold Falkner, who had been a pupil of Blomfield, was a friend of Miss Jekyll. Even though he had been 'trained from his early days in the ideas of the formal garden' he was almost won over to Jekyll's principles after visiting her garden at Munstead Wood which was 'partly formal, partly controlled wild'. She, however, moved to some degree towards formalism. Falkner says: 'In her first books she seemed to harp on naturalism in gardens in direct opposition [to *The Formal Garden*], but gradually she and E. L. [Edwin Lutyens] came to our way of thinking.'

As it was, both sides gave in to some extent. Falkner states that Miss Jekyll 'used to relate with great glee the fact that Robinson designed himself a garden all squares [Gravetye Manor], and Reggy a garden on a cliff with not a straight line in it [Point Hill]'.[15]

'A History of Renaissance Architecture in England, 1500–1800'

In 1892, the year that *The Formal Garden* appeared, Blomfield was approached by Messrs Bell, the publishers, and asked if he would write a history of English architecture. He rejected this suggestion, because 'the subject was far too big for one man',[16] but he did agree to tackle the period between 1500 and 1800. This was a period in which, of course, he was particularly interested, and his refusal to undertake a complete history probably underlines a desire to concentrate his effort upon the Renaissance, and not to waste it upon subject matter for which he had little enthusiasm. There was certainly a need for the book, for despite the trend towards a more literate and restrained classicism apparent in English architecture from the late 1880s onwards, no one had produced a history which comprehensively mapped the development of classical architecture in England.

Blomfield, as has been seen, had been collecting relevant material for some time, and the opportunity to work on so important a topic could not be missed, even though several more years were needed to complete the task, and it had to be written in parallel with a burgeoning architectural practice. It eventually appeared in 1897 in two volumes, and was immediately popular. An abridged version was soon proposed, and this 'short history' was intended to appeal to the student of architecture and the interested layman. It was in competition with J. Alfred Gotch's *Architecture of the Renaissance in England, 1560–1635* and Belcher and Macartney's *Later Renaissance Architecture in England*, which were well illustrated, but contained much less information and comment than Blomfield's volumes.

Blomfield's *History* is not a simple descriptive survey of a succession of styles. It is a personal account which seeks to demonstrate a main stream of tradition, the development of which reached a peak towards the end of the seventeenth century and, according to the author, decayed badly in the later years of the eighteenth century, with the growth of an eclectic and literary approach and the superficial desire for novelty and innovation at all costs. Blomfield adopts a highly critical position throughout. He endeavours to show where the main streams of development run, to point out that which is worthy and admirable, and that which is misguided and trivial. He illustrates the architecture that he admires, and boldly represents and analyses the English classical tradition which, by this time, formed the basis of his design philosophy. There can be no doubt, that in this book Blomfield is attempting to advocate and illuminate a tradition of good design which he would hope to reinstate.

The pattern of the book is similar to that employed in *The Formal Garden*, with a series of chapters dealing chronologically with movements and key architects, followed by sections on building techniques, planning and contemporary architectural literature. The brief conclusion allows for the pithy restatement of the major points and enables Blomfield to dwell upon the nature and qualities of English design, thereby reinforcing a theme that is present in nearly all of his written work.

Two architects stand out as heroes in Blomfield's book, Jones and Wren. He is scathing about many other well-respected names, and even Wren's work does not receive unqualified praise. In considering Wren, Blomfield writes:

> The special strength of Wren's genius lay in this largeness of idea, in this power of conceiving a great architectural scheme as a whole, of grasping it in complete perspective, and keeping his purpose proof against all the temptations of unnecessary detail.[17]

But of Inigo Jones he says:

> On the whole [he was] the greatest architect and one of the most accomplished artists that this country has produced. No man has mastered more completely the scholarship of his art; but to this range of knowledge he added a power of design and a quality of imagination which place him, as an artist, higher even than his great successor, Wren.[18]

He contrasts this approach with English architecture of the sixteenth century, the essential qualities of which were not related to the 'grand manner' which the book endeavours to promote, with its insistence upon scale, proportion and 'orderly distribution', but which relied upon 'accident of detail'. One cannot help but suppose that here Blomfield was using his historical account in order to provide a parallel with the position of the art in the late nineteenth century. For at least twenty years, English architecture had been dominated by the so-called 'Queen Anne' style which relied for its effect upon the com-

21 'The Banqueting House, Whitehall'. A drawing by Blomfield

bination of often disparate elements and details. In the hands of a master like Norman Shaw the outcome could be exciting and evocative. Lesser men often made a hash of it. Blomfield's generation felt the need of a design philosophy to replace this hit-and-miss eclecticism. In his *History* he draws the parallel and provides the solution to the problem.

Blomfield so enthusiastically espouses the 'grand manner' that it is difficult to believe that he was ever involved in the Arts and Crafts movement. The 'grand manner' demands that all considerations are subordinate to an overriding aesthetic concept; arts and crafts architects were generally concerned with the building's response to its location, the use of traditional materials and honesty of expression both in terms of function and construction. Blomfield's statement about the dome of St Paul's must have sounded like heresey to any of his Art Workers' Guild colleagues who were still faithful to their philosophy, though the Guild did encompass people of differing standpoints. However, the whole thing is given extra significance by the way in which it is written:

The brick cone which supports the lantern and cupola is an extremely skilful expedient, and an architect is not bound to show every detail of his construction, however ugly it may be. The ultimate justification of architecture is that it should be stable and beautiful. It is in the architect's discretion to choose his means of impressing the imagination, and, provided he attains his result, he is not to be bound by any pedantic

22 'Groombridge Place, Kent'. A drawing by Blomfield

23 'Eaves, Cornice and Quoin, Cranbourne'. A drawing by Blomfield

and irrelevant criticism as to his means – criticism, moreover, which assumes an intention which never existed in the architect's mind.[19]

The tradition engendered by Jones and Wren is greatly admired by Blomfield, but his praise is not confined to large-scale works, and he notes 'the kindly manner of domestic architecture inspired by Wren', an influence much in evidence in his own smaller works at this time.

There is plenty of harsh criticism of formalism not used as a means to an end, but as an end in itself. For instance, the British Palladians were scorned for what he considered to be their superficial achievements. The irony is heavy:

Palladio once made a skilful design of a villa for Monsignor Paolo Almerigo. . . . This villa was well adapted for a summer residence in a hot climate. It provided shelter from the blazing sun, and a free current of air in all directions, two qualities essential in Italy, but which exactly disqualified it for a country house in the damp cold atmosphere of the North. Notwithstanding, this design was so much admired by the aristocratic *virtuoso* of the eighteenth century that he was moved to transplant it entire to England, and Campbell duly reproduced Almerigo's villa at Mereworth. Chimneys would have spoilt the effect, and accordingly Campbell (who was certainly a most ingenious person) managed to get rid of his flues through the dome.[20]

The lucidity and sarcasm are typical of Blomfield's style, which makes amusing and informative reading. The whole work seems to have been written with tremendous enthusiasm and as a result it has vitality which most books with any pretence to scholarship tend to lack. The same feeling for the subject is apparent in Blomfield's drawings which are used, together with contemporary engravings, to illustrate the book.

The positive attitude taken by the author is engaging, and his views appear to be fervently held, though some may call this arrogance. All this is backed up by the impression of extensive scholarship. Blomfield's understanding of classical architecture appears to be very highly developed, as is his sense of taste, though this is not always borne out in his own buildings. His treatment of some of the revered names of eighteenth-century architecture is shocking, almost sensational, but it is consistent with his overall view of design: Vanbrugh 'had no taste'; the quality of Hawksmoor's imagination was 'ungraceful and ponderous'; 'William Kent was one of those generally accomplished persons who can do everything up to a certain point, and nothing well'; Robert Adam's ornamental innovations were 'wholly for the bad'.

The *History*, more than anything, established the direction Blomfield wished to take in his own building designs and to develop in subsequent writings. In terms of the advancement of his career it must be regarded as a work of enormous value, putting him into the forefront of architectural thought, in a period when serious thinking in architecture was conspicuously absent.

On a more practical level, both the *History* and *The Formal Garden* were instrumental in helping to 'open up' Blomfield's practice, and C. H. Reilly recollected: 'Sir Reginald once told me he traced the growth of his practice in early days largely to this book [i.e. *The Formal Garden*].'[21] Indeed, owners of country houses with formal gardens must have been pleased to find a young architect interested in their history, beauty and meaning. One result, typically, was that Sir Henry Edwardes of Wotton Hall, Derbyshire, consulted Blomfield about his garden, and he was later responsible for introducing his architect to Lord Yarborough, who gave Blomfield his 'first really important work', the rebuilding of Brocklesby Park.

Blomfield had travelled around visiting many great houses whilst preparing his *History* and he had become known to 'various excellent clients'. The visits were also important in building up a stock of architectural sources, so that although he was narrowing down his architectural vocabulary he was expanding his knowledge and the appreciation of its elements.

The writing of these two books in the 1890s, then, was useful in many ways and brought Blomfield to the forefront. His works were helpful to students of architecture and architects alike, but they were also of interest to the intelligent layman, and in this way he was introduced to a wider public.

CHAPTER 3
COUNTRY HOUSES

Blomfield believed that 'the design of houses in town and country is . . . the most attractive part of an architect's work,'[1] and his practice was dominated from the mid 1890s up to the outbreak of the First World War by domestic output. Although some of this was concerned with the design of fairly modest suburban houses, there were a large number of country-house commissions which came his way in increasing numbers following the publication of *The Formal Garden in England*. There were three main spheres of activity: the restoration and reordering of old buildings; the construction of entirely new buildings; and the design and alteration of gardens. In some cases, one commission would lead to another: called in to renovate the house, additions would be asked for and this would be followed by requirements for the provision of new gardens.

This kind of work suited Blomfield well. It brought prestige and contact with the wealthy and it was, indeed, ideal for the 'artist-architect', the man who wished to be above the hurly-burly of commercial practice and the necessity of submitting eye-catching or sycophantic schemes in competitions. As Sir John Summerson has pointed out:

> The private house-building sector flourished within a wide economic range, from the luxurious country mansion to the well-equipped suburban house in Wimbledon or Colinton and, between the two and perhaps most characteristic of the period, the house of moderate size designed for the enjoyment of wealth in retirement in favoured retreats like Haslemere or Helensburgh. Here, of course, the competition principle did not apply. Patronage was by recommendation and the architect's only obligations were to satisfy his client and please himself.[2]

Blomfield's country houses were built at a time when he was gradually adopting a more stable and sober architectural language, derived mainly from English buildings of the late seventeenth and early eighteenth centuries, and known facetiously as the 'Wrenaissance' style. None of his houses was extravagant by the Victorian standards of thirty or forty years before, and he was content with a limited palette of materials, mostly red brick and stone. He tried to make his houses part of the country scene instead of vulgar proclamations of the owner's wealth.

Blomfield was lucky that he was able to devote some twenty years of his life to this kind of practice, for the middle period of his career coincided with the final years of country-house building. The First World War, which presaged a change in social and economic conditions, killed the country house as effectively as it slaughtered the scions of the landed gentry.

Reordering and Restoration

Large houses often suffered neglect or destruction by fire. Sometimes wealthy new owners, and perhaps even tenants, taking over estates from the impoverished aristocracy, decided to sweep away the accretions of centuries and convert ugly and inconvenient old houses into handsome and comfortable modern mansions. The extent of the architect's involvement varied and may have been great or small. Sometimes work was piecemeal and took place over many years, at other times it was effected comprehensively and quickly.

The restoration of Heathfield Park, Sussex, dates from 1896–97. The house, originally built in 1677, but remodelled in 1766, was 'a rather ugly building. . . . Instead of facing south where there was a glorious view . . . the drawing room faced north, and the plan was extremely inconvenient.'[3] In order to correct this, and to realise the potential of house and site, Blomfield undertook an exacting schedule. He enlarged the house by seventy-five per cent, adding to the east side and rearranging the interiors. He refaced the building in new brickwork, introduced steel joists to replace the old timber binders, redesigned the elevations, replaced balustrades and cornices, and altered the position of the entrance.

Despite these efforts the appearance of the house promotes a feeling of

24 Heathfield Park, Sussex, as altered and enlarged. North front

unease. There are problems with symmetry, the roof is a jumble of hips and dormers and the walls are packed with windows. Like his early scheme at Brooklands, the restoration was obviously a difficult problem and he made the best of complicated and perhaps irreconcilable demands.

His expertise increased as he received more commissions of a similar kind and he was soon able to cope competently with large and complicated problems.

Brocklesby Park was, perhaps, the grandest renovation undertaken. It was the seat of Lord Yarborough, whose lands extended for some 40,000 acres in remote North Lincolnshire. Although the house was large it was not, as might be expected from so huge a domain, a great Palladian mansion. It was, in fact, an amalgam of work of different periods. The original building was Jacobean, but this was replaced in about 1730 by a block incorporating parts of the old house. Additions were made in the mid nineteenth century, but most of the house was gutted by fire in 1898, and at this stage Reginald Blomfield was called in.

Lord Yarborough came into contact with Blomfield through his friend, Sir Henry Edwardes. Sir Henry had consulted Blomfield about the design of his gardens at Wotton Hall in Derbyshire, and was so impressed by his architect that he unhesitatingly recommended him to Yarborough. A good working

25 Brocklesby Park, Lincolnshire, as restored. South front

relationship seems to have developed between architect and client, and Blomfield set about the tricky job of reconstructing and remodelling the house and gardens.[4]

Much of the Georgian east front of the building was left standing after the fire and this was built up anew where destruction had occurred. Its design sets the tone for the rest of the house which is, externally, very restrained in character: built of brick with stone dressings, it lacks the surface modulation usually provided by pilasters and ornament. Blomfield added two large single-storey bay windows, and an entrance vestibule to the south side of the house, but these accretions are all that break its plainness.

Despite the extensive remodelling of the south front, the entrance façade is not symmetrical and Blomfield's new vestibule is off-centre. Perhaps any attempt at symmetry would have been futile, as the south elevation of the western block is not uniform with that of the eastern block. This evident lack of symmetry is in conflict with the parterre, pools and formal driveway stretching in front of the south elevation.

Internally, the alterations caused some of the principal rooms of the house to be moved and others re-defined. Blomfield reconstructed the old great hall in the Georgian block, which was put to use as a dining room by Lord Yarborough. This grand room, occupying five bays and rising through two storeys, was one of the chief features of the remodelled house. Among other alterations, he converted the drawing room to a new entrance hall, formed a morning room off the hall, and ran a 'U'-shaped corridor around the inside of the house with a main staircase in the south-east corner. Decoration employed throughout, except for the great hall, was late seventeenth-century in style. Thus, the house was made more convenient internally, some of its finer features exploited to good effect and the interior scheme made consistent.[5]

Another large-scale restoration with similar objectives was at Chequers Court, Buckinghamshire. The house has become famous as the Prime Minister's country residence and is now simply known as 'Chequers'. Blomfield was called in by Bertram Frankland-Russell-Astley 'soon after the publication of *The Formal Garden in England* (1892)'.[6] Astley's first concern was the improvement of the gardens, and Blomfield designed a terrace to run along the south front of the house. It was not long, however, before he started to take an interest in the house itself, most of which dated from the mid sixteenth century, but with an exterior which had been Gothicised in the early nineteenth century. As Blomfield himself wrote:

The house at that date [1892] was extremely ugly, and very
inconvenient. It had been covered with stucco about a hundred years
ago, when the landscape gardeners were laying it down that red brick
was a blot on the landscape. I was wandering round the house, when

26 Brocklesby Park, Lincolnshire. The morning room

I came upon a piece of loose stucco and saw underneath it some beautiful brickwork . . . I called Astley's attention to this, and amid much enthusiasm the whole houseparty set to work picking off the stucco, and clearing about 100 square feet of fine brickwork like the older parts of Hampton Court.[7]

Thus was set in train a series of improvements which took place over many years. The building was gradually divested of its battlements, sash windows and other anachronistic features, but it was not until the tenancy of the distinguished politician Arthur Lee, which began in 1909, that substantial changes were made. Blomfield took the rambling circulation pattern firmly in hand and reorganised the service accommodation, converting the old kitchen and butler's pantry into a dining room. Previously, the kitchen had been located almost as far as could be from the dining room. He also concerned himself with the large central hall, which had been fitted out in the nineteenth century. He swept these features away and produced a more dignified and appropriate design, adding elements in sixteenth- and seventeenth-century styles. A new entrance court and porch were also constructed.

Returned to something more akin to its Tudor origins, the house was

51

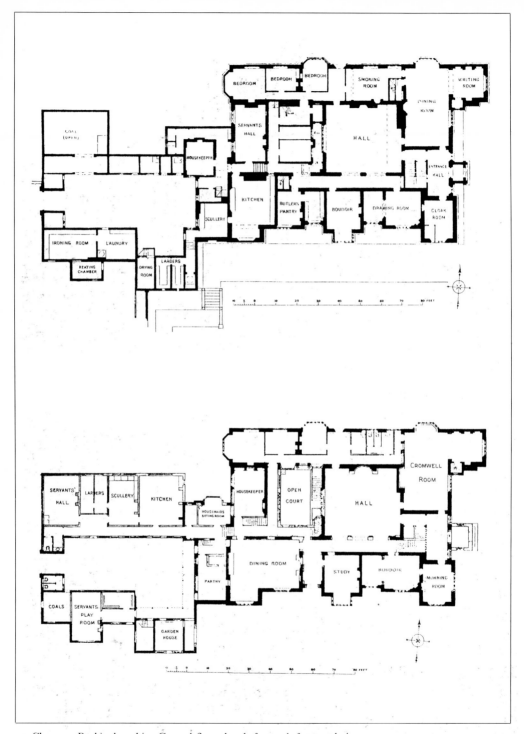

27 Chequers, Buckinghamshire. Ground-floor plans before and after reordering

28 Chequers from the north-east, showing Blomfield's new porch

29 Chequers. The Great Hall

30 Apethorpe Hall, Northamptonshire. South front

handed over to the nation in 1917 by Lee, who had previously purchased the property from the Astleys.[8]

It is clear that Blomfield had an eye for period detail, and one of his great strengths seems to have been spotting opportunities for the restoration of houses which had lost much of their original form or character over the years by the addition of fashionable contemporary details. In 1909 *Country Life* reports that at Apethorpe Hall in Northamptonshire,

> Mr. Blomfield has done much . . . both inside and out. But his work nowhere obtrudes itself. It is mostly confined to such necessary reparations and alterations as an old and somewhat neglected house calls for to fit it to the conditions of modern life. Every good, old feature, of whatever period it might be, has been preserved, and so the house retains its history.[9]

The same may be said for much other work, such as Knowlton Court and Godinton Park, both in Kent, Sulgrave Manor, Northamptonshire, and Milner Court, Kent, where he modestly altered the house and garden over a period of sixteen years. La Manoire de la Trinité, Jersey, though, is something of an oddity. Blomfield was employed to alter and enlarge the house in 1909, and he made it a much grander affair. He constructed substantial outbuildings and extensions, formed a *cour d'honneur* outside the main entrance and topped the building with a huge hipped French roof with two rows of dormers and tall chimneys. The result is a building of character and singularity, but completely different in scale to the original.

31 La Manoire de la Trinité in 1890, before alterations

32 La Manoire de la Trinité as altered and enlarged by Blomfield

There is no doubt that Blomfield developed an enviable competence, and his reputation for bringing a variety of country houses of all types and conditions back to life was well earned. His capacity for the design of new houses had also developed, and the first decade of the century, in particular, was a prolific period.

New Houses

Moundsmere Manor, Hampshire, is a splendid example of Blomfield's design work for new country houses in the early years of this century. It is quintessentially Edwardian, and although it cannot be said to be typical of his house designs, it vividly combines many of their representative qualities. There are 'Wrenaissance' details, although decoration is restrained and the house is rather more severe in its classicism than earlier buildings. It echoes the palace forms of Hampton Court, rather than those of the more humble late seventeenth-century country mansions, which were the usual sources of inspiration for Blomfield's domestic schemes. The scale, in fact, is rather deceptive, and the style of the building would lead one to expect something far larger. It is a sumptuous house and was, no doubt, expensive to build, but Jane Eyre's assessment of Thornfield Hall seems appropriate. It was, she wrote, 'a gentleman's house, not a nobleman's seat'.

The builder of Moundsmere, begun in 1908, was Wilfred Buckley, a lawyer of American origin who decided to devote himself to the advancement of the art of dairy farming. He acquired an estate of four hundred acres on the site of an ancient manor near Preston Candover in Hampshire and commissioned Blomfield to design the house, its gardens and various ancillary buildings. The setting in the quiet, rolling countryside is not spectacular, but the house and gardens complement each other and form an area of intensive design within the larger-scale pattern of farmland.

The main body of the house has a double-banked plan, with hall, staircase and cloakroom on its north side, and library, drawing room and dining room comprising the south side. From this, a wing containing the billiards room runs to the north, forming one side of the entrance court. The other side of the court is defined by a three-storey service wing. Further service areas together with this form a courtyard to the north-east of the house.

The ground-floor accommodation is not unusual for a house of its size and period. It is decorated mainly in a late seventeenth- or early eighteenth-century manner, a style rich enough to provide visual interest and an air of restrained wealth, without being cluttered. Some emphasis is given to the hall, a pleasant single-storey space, approximately half the width of the main block, which leads via an opening flanked by pairs of Ionic columns to the staircase. The first floor is, however, out of the ordinary. It is planned in

33 'Hampton Court, North East Corner'. A drawing by Blomfield

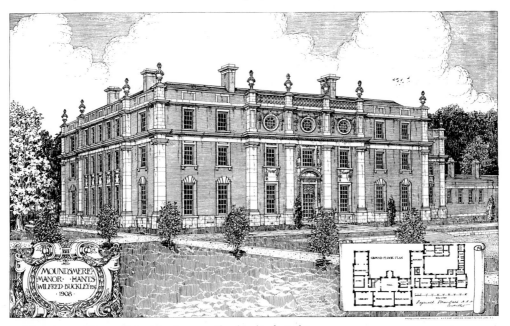

34 Moundsmere Manor, Hampshire. A perspective drawing from the south-west by James B. Fulton

accordance with American practice, whereby pairs of bedrooms are separated by a zone comprising a bathroom and a pair of 'walk-in closets'. The large number of bathrooms provided was unusual for an English country house, but perhaps the American owner was more hygiene-conscious – certainly his farm produced the first T.T. tested milk in Great Britain – and the bathrooms with their white tiled floors and walls and chromium-plated fittings have a surgical monumentality.

The upper floor is given over to the nursery, originally used to accommodate Mr Buckley's only child, Jenny, and her nursemaids.

Externally, the house is restrained and constructed in brick, with stone pilaster strips running to a cornice above first-floor level, and then continuing up through the attic storey and parapet to be terminated in stone urns. The central feature on the symmetrical, seven-bay south façade with its pilasters and round windows is very reminiscent of Wren's work at Hampton Court. The symmetry is further emphasised by the sunken garden and pool disposed about the axis of the south front. Unfortunately, Blomfield seems to have been unable or unwilling to continue and resolve the axiality in terms of planning. The centre line of the north front does not match that of the south, a problem brought about by the relative positions of the wings to the east and west of the entrance court. This discrepancy is, perhaps, only annoying to the theoretician, as it is not easily perceived in actuality.

35 Moundsmere Manor. Entrance hall looking towards the stairs

36 Wretham Hall, Norfolk. A photograph taken as the house neared completion

Moundsmere was designed for comfortable, rather than grand living and, in true Edwardian fashion, despite the stylistic references to a previous age, modern technology was fully employed. Electric lighting was used throughout, and fire hydrants occur on each floor. There was a hydraulic lift and central heating was provided, radiators being located in timber boxings beneath the window sills. Fresh air was healthily admitted through grilles in external walls and passed over the radiators as it entered the rooms. Despite this acceptance of labour-saving convenience and comfort, though, it must be admitted that at ground-floor level, at least, the area devoted to servants and their associated offices is as great as that used by the owner and occupier.[10]

Civilised and comfortable, Moundsmere sits gracefully in its farmland setting, surrounded by avenues of clipped yews and neat formal gardens.

Similar in style was Wretham Hall, near Thetford in Norfolk. It was built in 1913 for Saxton Noble, son of the industrialist, Sir Andrew Noble, and was, in fact, Blomfield's last large house. It was initially intended as a shooting box, but grew prodigiously, undergoing changes during the design period, one drawing showing it with high hipped roofs of almost French proportion. However, it reverted to the Moundsmere type in its final form, even though it was larger than its prototype. In this case, the problem of planning symmetry was revolved, the main house being an 'H' on plan, symmetrical about two axes. The overall impression was of a great mansion, the relationship of scale

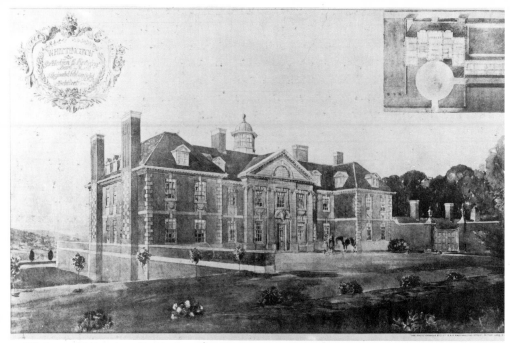

37 Wittington, Medmenham, Buckinghamshire. Entrance front, drawn by Stanley Adshead, 1909

and style perhaps being more appropriate here than at Moundsmere. Unfortunately it has been demolished, whereas Moundsmere survives as a family
home.[11]

An earlier house which was altered during its building and greatly expanded
shortly afterwards, is Wittington, near Medmenham in Buckinghamshire.
The final result is a suave essay in the late seventeenth-century style, which
Blomfield admired above all others for domestic design. Apart from Moundsmere and Wretham, Hampton Court derivatives are rarely to be found in
his houses, instead one has to look to buildings such as Belton House, Groombridge Place, Honington Hall, and Uppark, as probable sources of inspiration.
Blomfield's affection for houses of this type obviously informed the spirit of
Wittington, and despite the fact that it could never be mistaken for anything
other than an Edwardian house, direct parallels may be drawn. The original
version bore a marked resemblance to Groombridge Place, but in the final
scheme the north, or entrance front is very similar to that of Belton House,
with its projecting wings, hipped roofs, dormers and central lantern. The
number and disposition of bays is the same, as is the slightly projecting pedi-
mented central feature. Wittington's south front is more relaxed and less
derivative, however.

The house was constructed for Sir Hudson Kearley, who had built up gro-
cery businesses, including International Stores, pioneering the idea of
multiple shops. He was also a Member of Parliament and Chairman of the

Port of London Authority. Kearley's demands were obviously changeable. The original design dates from 1897 when Kearley purchased the freehold of the site from Oxford University. It was altered during building, yet soon further additions were planned and in 1909 the whole house was remodelled. The remodelling increased accommodation, but also altered the character of the house, making it more imposing. The drawing room was enlarged, and a library and study incorporated. This was achieved by the addition of wings attached to the east and west of the main block, which also had the effect of making the house symmetrical about a north-south axis.[12]

The general air of sumptuousness is increased by the gardens which are terraced down the valley side away from the house which stands at the summit of the slope. From a distance the dark green of the surrounding foliage encloses glimpses of the red brick and Ham Hill stone of the walls and chimneys, and the green Westmorland slate of the sweeping roofs. Lavish yet restrained, comfortable yet with more than a little formality, the whole scene could not be a more agreeable evocation of prosperous Edwardian life.

This mood is present, also, in Saltcote Place, Rye, a house built as a wedding present for a young member of the Hennessy family in about 1905. A much less resolved design than Wittington, it is a jolly jumble of elements, many of which it has in common with the larger house, with a pediment, full-width

38 Saltcote Place, Rye, from the east. The glazing to the loggia is not original

39 Caythorpe Court, Lincolnshire, from the south

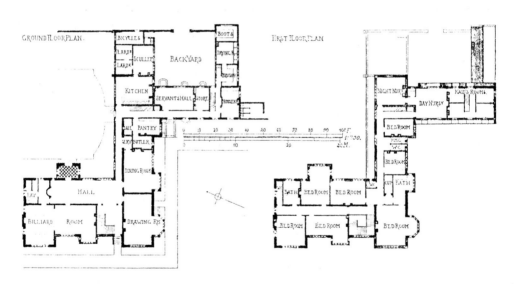

40 Caythorpe Court, ground-floor and first-floor plans

balcony and loggia beneath. Surrounded by rose gardens, a tennis court and a croquet lawn, it provides an excellent background to the lives of a wealthy young couple in the years before the First World War. A sale brochure of 1920 describes it aptly:

> The interior decorations of the residence are in perfect taste, and the appointments in every respect are on the best modern lines conducing to comfort and convenience. Electric light from a private plant is installed throughout. House telephones are connected to the principal rooms. Fire hydrants, with hose and appliances, are fitted on landings to the upper floor, and in the yard outside. A service lift runs from the basement to the top floor. Hot water radiators are fitted to the corridors and several rooms.[13]

Saltcote uses an architectural vocabulary common to many of Blomfield's houses. It was his preferred style yet, on occasions, he was prepared to move away from it. Caythorpe Court, Lincolnshire, is a case in point. Although it is somewhat earlier in date than the houses so far described, it does interrupt the flow of stylistic development which was to culminate in Wittington. Caythorpe has strong vernacular overtones. As *The Builder* put it: 'The design was, by desire, based on the plain seventeenth-century work as practised in Lincolnshire.'[14] In other words, the starting point and chief source for the design was the style of architecture developed over many years in that particular area, using local materials and techniques. Historically, it was the style that was swept away by the encroachment of classicism.

The house was built on the site of an old farm on high ground overlooking the Vale of Belvoir. Its wealthy owner, Major Edgar Lubbock, was a banker and brewery director, and master of the local hunt. Its purpose was to serve as a hunting lodge, and apart from the house there were stables containing no fewer than thirty loose boxes, coach houses and harness rooms. Blomfield undertook overall development of the site in one phase, building work commencing in 1899 and final completion occurring in 1901.

The walls are of Ancaster stone, with bands of local ironstone, and the roofs covered with Colyweston slates. Externally, the use of these materials generates a highly textured and relatively complex form with small gables and bays. Thus the overall appearance of the house is romantic, with its high gables, roofs, chimneys and mullioned windows, but there is a strong sense of visual order underlying it all. Oddly, the stables and ancillary buildings are, by contrast, in a cottagey arts and crafts style, with big, sweeping hipped roofs, massive chimneys and cupolas.

Internally, the decoration is in keeping with the general style and purpose of the house. Oak panelling and decorative plasterwork are much in evidence. The hall, for instance, has a frieze depicting pheasants, partridges and fruit

41 Wyphurst, Cranleigh, Surrey. A perspective drawing by James B. Fulton, 1907

trees. The ambience is pleasantly rural, but all the details appear to have been carefully worked out, down to such items as the radiator boxes.

The plan of Caythorpe is 'L' shaped, an entrance court being formed between the right-angled wings. Service accommodation is to the east, and at the junction between the cottagey servants' wing and the main house, Blomfield has used a chunky, rectilinear tower which is a feature which may be found in several of his houses. On the whole, the house is more modest than those so far described, with a much narrower hall and a tightening of circulation space. Notwithstanding this, the whole development of buildings and external works cost £120,000, a considerable sum in 1900. Part of the cost may be accounted for by the fact that building took place upon a glacial moraine, where the bearing capacity of the soil was not sufficient to take the weight of the structure on conventional strip foundations. Deep shafts were sunk, filled with load-bearing material and arched between, somewhat akin to a modern pile and ground beam system. It is clear from this and from other examples that Blomfield was prepared to used his ingenuity as far as technological problems were concerned, even though the architectural style was archaic.

C. E. H. Chadwyck-Healey's Wyphurst, Cranleigh, Surrey (1907), is another non-Wrenaissance house. It is, strictly speaking, an extension of an existing building, but the new work forms the main body of the house. Here Blomfield uses a 'Tudor' style, with patterned brickwork and shallow projecting bays. Despite the quaint details, the design seems to lack vigour, yet it must have been considered a major achievement, as, together with Moundsmere, it appears at the head of the report in the *RIBA Journal* recording the presentation of the Gold Medal to Blomfield in June 1913.

Whether 'Wrenaissance', Tudor or Jacobean, there is no doubt that Blomfield enjoyed the design and restoration of country houses and that they formed the single most significant part of his practice up to 1914.

More Gardens

In many cases, as has been seen, Blomfield designed gardens to complement houses. A fuller description may show how his ideas, outlined in *The Formal Garden*, were implemented. He believed that external as well as internal spaces should be considered by the architect and that they should all be part of a carefully controlled composition. This was particularly so in the case of completely new buildings. Caythorpe Court is an example. Built on high ground overlooking a valley, its gardens descend rather grandly in a series of lawn-covered terraces, buttressed by long walls. These walls are broken by flights of steps located on the central axis of the composition which is related to the centre-line of the south front of the house. In the angle between the house

42 A bird's-eye view of Caythorpe Court showing the gardens, stables and ancilliary buildings

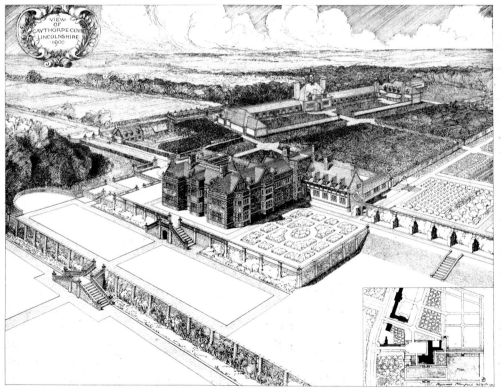

65

MELLERSTAIN
Col. Lord Binning CB
BIRDS EYE VIEW
Of NEW GARDENS from HOUSE to CANAL
DISTANCE FROM HOUSE TO CANAL 670 FEET, CANAL 1900 FEET X 400 FEET
Reginald Blomfield ARA Architect
invenit 1910.

and the service wing is a parterre, and then a high wall divides off the large kitchen garden to the north-east. The composition responds well to the house and its location. It provides a suitable context and setting for an important building.

The restoration of Apethorpe Hall brought with it the possibility of new designs for gardens and courts. There are broad avenues of trees and grand vistas, terraces with great sweeps of lawn, but also small, intimate spaces, such as the delightful millstone garden with its topiary and sunken pool. At Brocklesby Park, the gardens are also on a grand scale, water features playing an important part. There is a formal drive to the house along an avenue of clipped shrubs, running between two large pools and then up ramps between piers, surmounted by urns. On the axis of the entrance vestibule, at the far end of the vista, there is a sculptural focal point. A canal runs parallel with the east front of the house, though at a little distance, and two terrace levels lower. The peaceful symmetry of the garden, aided especially by the areas of water, helps to 'settle down' the unevenness of the house.

It was whilst searching for sculpture to use in the new gardens that Blomfield discovered the sculpture group of Neptune and Glaucus. It had lain in the Brocklesby orangery unrecognised for many years, and was now set up as a central feature. It was only later that he was able to verify it as the work of Bernini, dating from 1625.[15]

Blomfield's greatest garden project, however, was for Lord Binning at Mellerstain House in Berwickshire. Here terraced gardens with parterres and topiary were laid out on a very large scale to the south of the house. The terraces stepped down to a huge lawn, which in turn ran steeply down to the lake which had been enlarged by Blomfield. The design was not carried out in full for, as Blomfield ruefully notes in his *Memoirs*, although it was 'in the best manner of Lenôtre . . . it would have required the resources of Louis XIV to carry out the whole of my design.'[16]

Smaller-scale formal gardens were successfully re-instated at Godinton and Knowlton Court, both in Kent. At Godinton new yew hedges were planted, a rose garden established and a fish pond created. The spirit of the old geometric garden was revived. Similarly, at Knowlton, where it was found upon excavation that the boundaries of Blomfield's new scheme coincided exactly with the footings of the old garden walls, splendid sunken gardens and terraces were established. Here, as elsewhere, Blomfield did not neglect details. Gates, walls, sundials, balustrades and other incidentals help to reinforce the feeling created by the scheme as a whole.[17]

Sometimes more unusual details were also favoured. At Milner Court, Kent, for instance, there was a charming brick gazebo and a remarkable wooden bridge, which had a distinctly oriental appearance, spanning the River

43 A bird's-eye view of the proposed gardens at Mellerstain, drawn by Adrian Berrington

44 Knowlton Court, the terrace from the sunken garden

45 Knowlton Court, Kent, from the south-east, showing the sunken garden

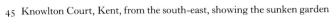

Stour. Sculptural forms were also introduced in certain gardens both to act as focal points and as foils to the vegetation.

There is no doubt that the quality of Blomfield's gardens is high, and that their design shows a deep feeling and sensitivity for formal landscape, as may be expected from the author of, perhaps, the leading book on the subject. He did not achieve the heights of creativity attained by Lutyens and Jekyll, but he usually managed to create an appropriate setting and ambience for his houses and to carry through a clear and consistent design theme.

Many will regard Blomfield's houses and gardens as his best architectural work. Despite his predilection for the 'grand manner' and large-scale urban design, it may be that he was at his most relaxed and most able in modest and restrained country settings. Like so many of his contemporaries, particularly those of the Shaw circle, he responded most fully to the English country scene.

CHAPTER 4
PROFESSIONAL INVOLVEMENTS

Blomfield was very firmly established in practice by 1900. At the age of 43, he was well known for his two distinguished books, his country houses and a variety of other projects. He had been involved with major art movements in the 1880s and 1890s and was associated with several of the leading figures in the world of the visual arts. The early years of the twentieth century, however, saw Blomfield and many of his colleagues moving away from their radical associations.[1] They began to enter the 'established' organisations where they assumed important and influential rôles, and by the time the First World War broke out Blomfield was one of the central pillars of the architectural 'establishment'.

There was no sudden desertion of one camp for another. Increasing conservatism and the onset of middle age may have had something to do with it, but Blomfield had long been involved with official bodies. His interest in education and his feelings about the architect's rôle as an artist, rather than a professional, stretched back to the early Shaw 'family' days, and these were the topics that precipitated his involvement in the RIBA and the Royal Academy. In some respects, even within these bodies, he remained a radical. He shook them up, and thought of himself as a reformer rather than a consolidator.

Before examining his involvement more closely, it is necessary to go back to earlier years when his interest in professional politics first became apparent.

The Memorialists

In the debates about professionalism and the rôle of the RIBA that took place in the late 1880s Blomfield had allied himself to those colleagues who considered themselves to be 'artist-architects'. Their attitude was that to belong to a profession was almost as disreputable as being involved in trade. Architecture was the mistress of the arts, and the architect should not be a mere business-minded professional, but an artist of considerable ability. It was, they thought, futile to attempt to close the profession to all but those who had passed a qualifying examination, because art was inexaminable.

There was, at the same time, a general feeling, particularly among provincial architects, that some sort of registration through compulsory examination was necessary in order to guarantee competence, this being one of the mainstays of the professional concept. Various moves were made by the Society of Architects, a body set up to press for statutory registration, culminating in the presentation of a Parliamentary Bill in 1891. This was opposed by the RIBA, but as Blomfield pointed out, 'it appeared from speeches by prominent members of the Institute, that they opposed it because they contemplated a scheme of Registration of their own, and that this was intimately connected with the Examination system of the Institute.'[2] In the words of T. G. Jackson, 'this time Norman Shaw took it up hot'.[3]

Shaw had considerable influence, and many of the most famous artist-architects followed his lead. Jackson notes:

> At Shaw's instance a few architects met at Mervyn Macartney's house at the corner of Berkeley Square to consider what should be done. I was invited and there I met Norman Shaw for the first time. It was decided to send a protest to the Institute stating our views, and to get it signed as widely as possible by artists of all kinds who sympathized with us.[4]

All of the Shaw 'family', of course, signed the Memorial, along with other distinguished architects and artists including Sir Arthur Blomfield, J. M. Brydon, Beresford Pite, J. O. Scott, J. J. Stevenson, William Butterfield, Basil Champneys, Philip Webb, Alma-Tadema, Holman Hunt, Burne-Jones and William Morris. The Memorial was published in *The Times*. The main crux of its argument was: 'We believe that, while it is possible to examine students in construction and matters of sanitation, their artistic qualifications, which really make the architect, cannot be brought to the test of examination. . . We think that no legislation can protect the public against bad design.'[5] These arguments were similar to those already stated in a letter to the RIBA, criticising its examination system, which had been written in 1889, and signed by Jackson, Shaw and Blomfield among others.

In reply to the Memorial, the RIBA stated that they sympathised with the Memorialists and had no intention of making architecture a 'closed' profession. The Memorialists, though, were not satisfied with the reaction of the RIBA, and after some futile discussion Blomfield stated that no compromise was possible, and that the only thing to do was to fight.

Blomfield, together with Mervyn Macartney, had acted as secretary to the Memorialists, and they and several other Shaw 'family' members of the Institute resigned. In the ensuing struggle Blomfield acted as 'aide-de-camp and general liaison officer' to Shaw and Jackson, and in 1892 a volume of essays was published with the title *Architecture : A Profession or an Art?* Shaw and Jackson edited the volume and Blomfield was among the thirteen contributors.[6] His essay was entitled 'Architecture and the Royal Institute of British Architects'. Sarcastically, he explained that the RIBA examination was 'framed with careful reference to a dead level of mediocrity'.

The stance taken was subsequently to be developed by Blomfield in later writings, such as *The Mistress Art*, but was admirably stated in Shaw and Jackson's publication: 'It is time that the public should place the architect in his proper place, namely at the head of the arts, where he should be, and not endeavour to thrust him to the tail of the professions.'[7]

The efforts of the Memorialists proved to be successful, and little was positively achieved in terms of Registration until the 1920s. However, during the intervening years the issue was kept alive, and, as will be seen, Blomfield was closely involved with the problems of Registration in the years leading up to the First World War.

Having resigned from the professional body, Blomfield remained outside its bounds until 1906. In the meantime, he built up his practice and expanded his scholarly and literary activities. His understanding and appreciation of classicism deepened, and he became very interested in the French tradition. This, in turn, had implications in terms of architectural education, and it was this subject that occupied much of his attention during the first decade of this century.

Education

Blomfield's developing architectural philosophy, which included the championing of the 'grand manner' and his admiration for the French Beaux-Arts system, helped to bolster and clarify his interest in architectural education. He felt that it was disorganised, half-hearted and without any proper goal. Examinations for membership of the RIBA, at first voluntary and later compulsory, had been held for several years, but the course of study leading to them was ill-defined and haphazard.[8] Part-time classes were held for articled pupils, and a few full-time schools had appeared, but there was little co-ordination between these various centres. Clearly, the system was in need of organisation.

The movement for the reform of education was crystallised in 1904. Blomfield and some other eminent non-Institute architects, such as W. R. Lethaby, Mervyn Macartney and Halsey Ricardo began the move by presenting a memorandum on education to the RIBA Council in 1903. Aston Webb (1849–1930), President of the RIBA and an accomplished and important architect whose professional skill Blomfield much admired, persuaded the Institute and non-Institute architects to work together, and by June 1904 a Board of Architectural Education had been appointed. Webb was chairman, Basil Champneys vice chairman, and Blomfield and John Slater honorary secretaries. In addition there were twelve other members drawn from the RIBA, the Architectural Association and the non-Institute architects. The initial deliberations of the Board were presented in a paper given by Blomfield in February 1905.[9] The paper summarised the historical and present position of architectural education, attempted to define what was needed to improve standards and suggested a mode of study and a common syllabus which could be applied in schools of architecture. The function of the Board was to act as a central advisory body and to provide Visitors to the educational establishments to ensure that standards were maintained. Soon, the Visitors were appointed, Blomfield being paired with Leonard Stokes, an Institute stalwart. C. H. Reilly, Head of the Liverpool School of Architecture, remembered the instigation of the visits. Blomfield, Mervyn Macartney and John Slater were among those attending. More specifically, he says:

> In those days Blomfield was very friendly to, and a great supporter of, the Schools of Architecture in general and of Liverpool I like to think, in particular. . . . In the early days of the School, before the [First World] war his stimulating visits were things to which my wife and I looked forward with great pleasure. So were those of his gentle successor, Ernest Newton.[10]

Blomfield also had a small number of articled pupils of his own, but despite his concern for educational matters his treatment of them differed little from that meted out by other architects. He delegated little but the most menial work, and his life was so busy that he had hardly any time to instruct them. G. Berkeley Wills, who was articled to Blomfield, remembered:

> We really got little personal instruction from Blomfield. One picked up what one could about building design, how to run an office and how to deal with clients by observation, questioning the chief assistant and visiting the various jobs whenever we could. Blomfield used to dash into our room, see what we were doing, urge us to attend the Academy Schools, or perhaps raise Cain about some mislaid drawings, depart like a whirlwind to meet a client – peace would once more descend on the office. Some of us tried to add to our eduction by attending evening classes at the Polytechnic, but I was the only one taking the RIBA examination for Associates at that time and to stay on as an assistant for about eighteen months.[11]

Blomfield's method of educating pupils seemed very simple and required the minimum of effort. Berkeley Wills wrote:

> When I first started my articles Blomfield gave me the whole of the drawings of a house he was building called 'Ballard's Court' at Goudhurst in Kent, and told me to take tracings of them, asking his chief assistant or one of the other pupils about anything I did not understand. When I had done this he sent me down to inspect the house

which was just then being completed. This was an excellent introduction to architecture and architectural drawing.[12]

No doubt, Blomfield was extremely busy, not only with his practice and his writings, but also with the Board of Architectural Education.

The close educational contact with the RIBA must have provided the necessary stimulus for Blomfield and his old colleagues from the Shaw 'family' to rejoin the Institute. This happened in 1906, and thus the 'Memorial' renegades of fifteen years earlier returned to the fold, many to become important establishment figures. They included Lethaby, Macartney, Newton and Horsley, all, Blomfield claims, 'led by myself'. He was made a Fellow of the Institute in the same year.

Blomfield's return to the RIBA was also politically motivated. He felt that he should support Aston Webb and his followers against the registrationists. Many of those returning signed a resolution:

> We feel that in rejoining the Institute we should clearly define our position:
> a) We understand that the RIBA will zealously support the scheme of Architectural education;
> b) We are strongly opposed to any legislative restrictions in the practice of Architecture.[13]

These political changes went hand in hand, to some extent, with changes in architectural philosophy. Some of the older men seem to have been left behind, while the others modified their youthful enthusiasms. This is dramatically underlined by a letter which Blomfield wrote to T. G. Jackson in April, 1906. Blomfield had been notified of his appointment as Professor of the Royal Academy School and Jackson wrote to him suggesting that there should be lectures on arts and crafts topics. 'I have come to the conclusion', Blomfield replied, 'that the Arts and Crafts Movement has done more harm than good to Architects.'[14]

The idea of a 'Final School' providing an 'advanced course in architectural training' seems to have been a hobby-horse for Blomfield. He championed the system when he succeeded Aston Webb as Chairman of the Board of Architectural Education and he proposed that the Advanced School, which he hoped would be centred on the Royal Academy, would carry on the training of the more promising students from the point at which the ordinary schools left off.[15] He also suggested that applicants for the Rome Scholarship should be from the Advanced School. To this end, the Academy School would require 'complete remodelling'. There was, at that time, according to Blomfield, no clear pattern of work. Subjects were set by the Visitors, and not enough importance was given to 'large conception in design'. Existing standards were far too low and he suggested that all candidates for entry to the Advanced School should be required to have passed the RIBA Intermediate Examination.

This proposal was put to the schools of architecture, but they were divided on the issue. Also in that year, 1910, Blomfield was passed over for election as a full member of the Royal Academy. He gave up, at least for the time being, his 'Final School' idea, complaining bitterly in a letter to Aston Webb: 'I had hoped to tackle the reorganisation of the Architectural School at the Academy in person, but had no intention of wasting time in attempting this through other men as intermediaries.'[16]

This was not the end of the 'Final School' idea and it cropped up again at least twice, though in different circumstances.

First, as a member of the Standing Committee of Advice to the Board of Education on Art Training he urged a final school of fine arts in the Royal College of Art. There would be new buildings, a new organisation and a new full-time school of architecture. Money would be provided by the State. The idea came to nothing, however, as Blomfield says that the academy did not care for State interference and the State could not make a positive decision. Second, in 1912 there was an attempt to introduce the atelier system. This was, of course, completely in accord with new architectural thinking and reflected Beaux-Arts influence. Blomfield backed it up, but said in an address given to the Architectural Association that an atelier without a final school was a 'cart without a horse', and as a final school could not be agreed upon the whole notion was given up.[17] It reappeared after the First World War and two ateliers were actually established, but the system failed.

After the war, Blomfield's interests and involvements changed. He had, however, been instrumental in setting up and influencing the new pattern of architectural education. He had also acted as a catalyst in stimulating discussion and had provided, at the very least, food for thought for all those involved in educating potential architects.

The Institute and the Academy

Involvement with the Board of Architectural Education was one way in which Blomfield became an indispensable member of the RIBA. His progress through the ranks was rapid. Upon rejoining the Institute in 1906 he was made a Fellow, quickly became a Council member, then Vice President, and by 1912 was President. He almost became President in 1910, in fact, and ran against Leonard Stokes (1858–1925), 'an Institute man pure and simple', but 'uncertain in temper and quite uncompromising in manner'.[18] Blomfield was senior Vice President when Stokes's health broke down in 1911 and he took over the work from January 1912 until his election in July of that year.

One of the main issues during Blomfield's Presidency was the perennial topic of registration. He expended a great deal of time and energy in coping with this problem but, like so many of his efforts in public life, after much struggle it ended without a positive result. He had often spoken against registration, but as it was Institute policy it was his duty to see it through and pressure was being brought from the provinces for the formulation of a Registration Bill.

In his opening Presidential Address to the RIBA in November 1912, Blomfield made it clear that registration was to put a stop to incompetence and 'to establish and maintain a reasonable level of accomplishment.'

He maintained, however, that personal merit was the most important thing and that registration in itself was not good enough. The concept of the artist-architect was still uppermost in his mind and he maintained that 'first of all we are artists'.[19]

The first report of the RIBA Council (1913) recommended the registration of architects, but statutory implementation seemed a remote prospect at the time, as there were constitutional difficulties and the expense incurred in promoting a Bill was very great. After further discussions it was decided that in order to solve the constitutional problems the RIBA would try to obtain a new charter whereby 'Chartered Architects' would be those who were qualified and approved by the Council of the RIBA. This proposal was put before the RIBA general assembly in 1914. There had been several difficult meetings beforehand, at which time complex issues had been thrashed out; Blomfield had as he put it 'held the reins' for these, but the whole business, he said, was 'knocked on the head' by the outbreak of the First World War, and ended inconclusively.[20]

Blomfield's two-year Presidency had come to an end with the debate on the registration proposals, but the Council asked him to stay on for a third year. To this he at first agreed, but shortly afterwards he suffered a breakdown and went away to recuperate on Admiral Sir George Warrender's flagship, which was lying in Weymouth Bay.[21] He was succeeded by Ernest Newton, a contemporary and 'stepbrother' in the Shaw 'family'.

Despite the futile efforts connected with the Registration Bill proposals, the Presidency of the RIBA had some tangible benefit for Blomfield. In the course of serving upon various committees he became involved in two large-scale urban design projects. One of these, concerning the completion of the Quadrant, Regent Street, marked an important stage in his career and forms part of the subject matter of Chapter 6. The other, the design for the approach to Admiralty Arch, was part of Aston Webb's grand scheme whereby Buckingham Palace was linked to Trafalgar Square by a great processional route running down the Mall. One of the major elements in the approach from the square was Drummonds Bank, designed by a previous RIBA President, George Aitchison. It was first proposed that in order to complete Webb's design alterations would have to be made to Drummonds building. Drummonds objected strongly to this and the impasse was eventually resolved when Blomfield designed a building to complement Aitchison's on the other side of the road, the main route passing between the two.

Blomfield was awarded the Gold Medal of the Royal Institute of British Architects in 1913. His reputation was high on the Continent, as well as at home. In May 1914, for instance, he opened an exhibition of British architecture in Paris, was fêted by the French, and was about to be made a member of the Légion d'honneur, but the award was blocked by the British Foreign Office. He seems, though, to have maintained contact with Continental and also American architects throughout his professional life.

The RIBA was not the only institution in which Blomfield demonstrated an ambition for position and power. The Royal Academy was an even greater target. Few architects achieved the status of full membership of the Academy, and Blomfield not only set his sights upon this goal, but upon the Presidency also. It is unfair to think of this as purely personal ambition, for he was concerned about the low number of architects in the Academy and was keen to reform membership.

Blomfield's first close contact with the Royal Academy, apart from his student attendance at the School, was achieved when he was elected an Associate in 1905. This was followed in 1906 by his appointment as Professor of Architecture, in succession to George Aitchison. The Instrument of Foundation of the Academy stated that the Professor should read six public lectures each year, 'calculated to form the taste of the Students'. Blomfield now had a base from which to propound his ideas about the 'grand manner'. The lectures that he gave at the Royal Academy School were in fact used as the basis for a very successful book, *The Mistress Art*, which was popular and influential in Great Britain and overseas.[22] It helped to reinforce Blomfield's reputation in middle age and to keep him to the forefront in matters of architectural theory.

By all accounts, Blomfield was an interesting lecturer, and this was particularly emphasised by the fact that he followed Aitchison, who had a very dry style. His objectives in giving the lectures were re-stated in the *Memoirs*:

> My idea was not to weary them [the students] with technicalities or too much history, but to endeavour to direct their attention to Architecture and the Arts in relation to life, as an expression of man's intelligence and imagination and as a means of realising himself.[23]

He endeavoured to carry out this aim for four years, but resigned in 1911 and was not replaced.[24]

During the following year Blomfield was busy as President of the RIBA, but in 1914, shortly before his term of office was due to come to an end, he was elected a full member of the Academy. This was a considerable honour and he joined T. G. Jackson and Aston Webb, the only other architects who were full members, in what was mainly a painters' preserve. Sir Edward Poynter was President and despite some initial conflict Blomfield was soon a respected and active member of the Council.

In the years following the First World War, Blomfield found himself involved in many of the committees set up by the Academy, but the story of his involvement belongs further on in this book.

It is valuable, though, to look at the published result of Blomfield's Academy lectures, for *The Mistress Art* represents a clear statement of his views on design and architectural education. It was influential upon a whole generation of aspiring architects.

'The Mistress Art'

The Mistress Art appeared in 1908 and, as in the collection of essays *Studies in Architecture* published three years earlier, the subjects discussed are somewhat diverse, but here emphasise design ideals and the nature of the 'grand manner'. Blomfield's task was to communicate to students, and in doing this he has left an account of his own mature approach to architecture. The basis of this was the use of a consistent classical language which was to be applied with imagination and was to reflect the temperament of the individual architect. He was at pains to point out that architecture was a rigorous intellectual discipline based upon sound scholarship and a knowledge and appreciation of existing examples. It was 'a grim intellectual art, and students should be well aquainted with certain key examples'. The work of Wren, for instance, is cited as an important subject for study: 'Probably no architect ever possessed a clearer brain or more ready resource than Wren, and I recommend to you the analytical study of the interior of his churches as an excellent training in simple architectural form.'[25]

Coupled with the acquisition of knowledge, there should be an appreciation of beauty. Blomfield maintains that 'if a building, however pedantically logical, is hideous to the eye, there is no more to be said about it, so far as architecture is concerned.' Moreover, standards of beauty are immutable: 'Our sense of beauty with all its limitations and imperfections has been built up by countless generations . . . artists may be justified in taking it for granted that certain things will always be considered beautiful and certain things ugly.'[26] This belief in an absolute standard of beauty led him to take issue with much nineteenth-century architecture, where he felt that questions of morality and the influence of ideas that really belonged to literature had perverted architectural effort. He thought that the highest expression of architecture was to be found in the 'grand manner' as represented in Egypt, Greece and Rome and, perhaps most relevantly, seventeenth- and eighteenth-century France. Here the conditions necessary for the production of great art were met.

Throughout the book there are statements about the 'grand manner' which help in an understanding of what Blomfield was attempting to propagate (but often failing to achieve in his own buildings) before the First World War. In the 'grand manner', he wrote, 'the greater efforts of architecture are obtained through scale, through orderly distribution, through a certain abstract and impersonal simplicity of treatment.' Again, 'the central idea is predominant everywhere, it is never sacrificed to detail.' Embodied in the 'grand manner' is 'an intellectual conception, far-reaching in its range and unfaltering in its purpose', and there is a 'lofty ideal and a power of imagination that rises superior to the entanglement of detail.'[27]

This impersonal and cool intellectual approach does not rule out the expression of the personality of the artist, however: 'Reason and the dry light of the intellect will not explain everything in this art . . . Temperament, no less than imagination and intelligence, is an essential element in good architecture.' Blomfield uses Peruzzi as an example. In his work he finds 'a masterful freedom which proves once for all that the talk of the tyranny of the Classic is either the result of ignorance or the confession of incompetence.'[28]

Although most of *The Mistress* Art is taken up with philosophical discourse, Blomfield does not neglect to mention something which is generally taken for granted in his writings, but which is shown to good effect in his buildings. That is the importance of a thorough knowledge of sound and appropriate building techniques. In Chapter 3, for instance, there is a statement about the relationship of technology to art: 'The science of the architect is the technique that enables him to express himself freely and faultlessly as an artist in building.' And later he remarks that 'the study of buildings and materials is, to the architect, what the study of anatomy is to the sculptor.'[29]

These statements indicate the path that Blomfield advised his students and the profession to take. It was an approach that was extensively propagated and one that the new full-time schools of architecture found especially appealing. Charles Reilly, Head of the University of Liverpool School of Architecture, said that the School's teaching was based on Sir Reginald's and that his books were textbooks for professors and students alike. It was due to Blomfield's influence that the orders were once again thoroughly studied.[30]

Blomfield's ideas were expressed at an opportune time as far as newly emerging architectural education was concerned. Full-time schools such as those at Liverpool, Glasgow and Manchester were becoming well established, and here was an approach to design that could be taught and which required an academic approach likely to endear itself to institutions of higher education. This was well-nigh impossible with the 'Free Style' and vernacular-influenced arts and crafts styles which were still popular. There was some talk of the 'tyranny of the classic' and Voysey called the Beaux-Arts approach 'a crutch for fools', but Blomfield saw the 'grand manner' as capable of providing a framework in which the individual temperament and imagination of the artist could be brought into play, and therefore his much loved concept of the 'artist-architect' was preserved and even enhanced.

Thus, the 'grand manner' became the successful 'school' style, and very soon most young architects who had passed through full-time education were using a fairly severe and consistent classical language with simply shaped, massive buildings planned around axis lines. Architecture was seen in terms of plans, sections and elevations and often high-quality presentation drawings were an end in themselves rather than illustrations of proposed buildings.

The success of the approach advocated by Blomfield, however, was not solely due to the spread of full-time education. The classical style was admirably suited to the new building types that were emerging at the turn of the century, or, at least, more suited than any of the other available styles. Municipal buildings were sprouting everywhere. Public libraries, council offices, fire stations, public baths and art galleries were developing in urban areas across the country, as were large-scale commercial buildings such as department stores and office blocks.

The 'grand manner', with its concept of urban design was ideal, because 'Free Style' and 'cottagey' styles could not be expanded to fit the necessary scale without appearing ridiculous. Rectilinear classical forms, also, were suitable for clothing steel frames which were making possible the larger spans and greater heights needed in new building types.

The new classicism, therefore, became a widely used style. Blomfield, of course, was only one of many protagonists, but he succeeded most ably in presenting a clear case, crystallising many of the views then held, and providing a scholarly historical background. The importance of others in propagating this classicism, though, should not be diminished. Reilly and Richardson did so through their teaching, and Mervyn Macartney turned *The Architectural Review*, under his editorship, into a journal which promoted sensitive classicism.[31] Should an individual be chosen, however, to represent the movement in all its aspects, then it must surely be Reginald Blomfield.

CHAPTER 5
DEVELOPING CLASSICISM: 1890 – 1914

The practice that was built up before the First World War was dominated by the country house, as has been shown in Chapter 3, but it was not solely dependent upon it. Blomfield was always a general practitioner; he designed small houses, educational buildings, public buildings and ecclesiastical work. There are one or two exceptions to his developing use of the classical language of design, but the main trend is increasingly towards restraint. The architectural vocabulary is usually taken from late seventeenth-century England, but is supplemented after the turn of the century by a number of schemes showing French influence.

In the main, for his larger buildings, Blomfield attempted to follow the precepts outlined in *The Mistress Art*.

The Smaller House

The architect's own house, and permanent base, 51, Frognal, Hampstead, is a rather understated piece of work, perhaps surprisingly so in view of the ebullient character of its occupant. It forms one half of a pair of semi-detached houses (numbers 49 and 51) built in 1892. The site was suggested by the man who became Blomfield's next-door neighbour, T. J. Cobden Sanderson, a fellow member of the Arts and Crafts Exhibition Society and a distinguished bookbinder and printer. Today the houses appear unremarkable, but when originally built they must have seemed 'cottagey' and 'arty'. They are of red brick with sweeping tiled roofs, hipped dormers and a 'Queen Anne' gable at each end, containing the Venetian-window motif often found in Blomfield's small-scale work at that time. They are among the first representatives of a personal style that had emerged from the welter of eclecticism apparent in his earlier years.

The 1890s, in fact, were the heyday of the small house in Blomfield's practice, and the restraint shown at Frognal is apparent in most of the other designs. There is a restricted palette of materials, motifs and elements to be seen in the houses built on the Burra Estates in Rye, such as Point Lodge, Playden. It may also be seen at Swiftsden and Hillside, Hurst Green, Sussex. Many of the cottages and lodges associated with great estates, and built well into the early years of this century, are similarly treated, but are usually constructed in the materials established for the estate as a whole. Individual houses are generally simple, plain red brick forms, often with stone quoins and dressings, small-paned vertical sliding sash windows, hipped roofs and handsome rectangular chimneys.[1]

46 Nos 49 and 51, Frognal, Hampstead, semi-detached houses for Cobden Sanderson and Blomfield

47 'Hill Side', Hurst Green, Sussex. View from the south-east

The Blomfield holiday home, Point Hill, Rye is in marked contrast. Begun in the mid 1890s, it contradicts practically all of Blomfield's architectural theories, but it is very successful in its informality. It is a house in which the site is of great importance, and it was chosen for that particular reason.

Whilst playing cricket at Rye, Blomfield spotted an old cottage high up on an inland cliff. Though perched rather precipitously it overlooked impressive views of the ancient port of Rye and out across Romney Marsh. He purchased the cottage and land, and the building was gradually expanded and altered no less than five times, until by 1912 it had become 'a comfortable little house with nine bedrooms and three bathrooms'.[2] The Blomfield family, which by the late 1890s consisted of Reginald Blomfield, his wife Frances and their three children Henry, Austin and Isabella, spent much of the summer here. When they were not in residence the house was let and at one time the American novelist Henry James was an occupant.

The house is approached from a steep, narrow lane bounded by high hedges. A gravel forecourt is entered, but the visitor is presented with a blank and mysterious wall, through which doors lead to the interior and the garden. No hint is given as to what may be found on the other side. The full extent of the house, indeed, can only be seen from the garden. It is a picturesque jumble of walls, chimneys, gables, hips and dormers. The observation turret is a curious feature, often used by Blomfield as a workroom. The architect bolted the access hatch and sat above it so that he would not be disturbed

48 Blomfield's drawing of the lodge, Caythorpe Court

49 Point Hill, sketched by Blomfield on the back of an envelope

50 View of Point Hill, showing its *ad hoc* qualities

by intruders. Materials seem to have been used on a rather *ad hoc* basis, and include rendered and plain brickwork, weather-boarding and tiles.[3] There are many references to local vernacular details.

The garden was built down the slope of the cliff, exploiting its precipitous nature by creating tortuous paths and overhangs. At the top, immediately next to the house, there was a hint of formality, with a fish pond and lawn tennis court, but everything else, with the exception of the gazebo area at the base of the cliff, was romantic and 'natural'. It was alive with the song of birds, and fruit trees and vines flourished on the south-facing slope.

The overall result of the building and its grounds is whimsical for, as Blomfield said, he 'came to Rye for sport and amusement.'[4]

Educational Buildings

Buildings for educational establishments formed a significant part of Blomfield's output from the earliest days. The Bradby Memorial Hall at Haileybury was followed by other work at that school as well as at Sherborne; there were important commissions for Goldsmith's College, London, and Lady Margaret Hall, Oxford, as well as smaller-scale school buildings. Many of these commissions enabled Blomfield to develop his 'Wrenaissance' style and apply it to large buildings.

One instance of this is a design submitted in a limited competion in 1896 for the proposed Girls' School, at Brook Green, Hammersmith.[5] This scheme has a symmetrical main façade, with projecting wings on either side. Located on the axis of the main entrance is the hall, surrounded by classrooms. The style adopted is full-blown 'Wrenaissance'. There are hipped roofs, lanterns, balusters, expanses of fairly plain brick wall punctuated by simple rectangular openings and 'pavilions' with more elaborate windows, segmental pediments and stone dressings.

The style was certainly considered suitable for Lady Margaret Hall. This Oxford college for women was founded in 1879, and its earliest buildings were by Basil Champneys. By 1896 it had been decided that there should be a planned and gradual expansion, and Blomfield first designed the Wordsworth building as the south block in the new complex. It contained twenty-eight student rooms and also common rooms. The north wing was to provide similar accommodation, whilst the link building was to contain a dining room and kitchen, a library and offices. Growth took place over many years, the south block being built in 1896, the link in 1904–5 and the north wing in 1914. The south block was extended in 1926 to form, with the link, two sides of a quadrangle.[6]

The materials which Blomfield used – red brick, Clipsham stone and tiled roofs – are consistent throughout, but the architectural vocabulary is modified

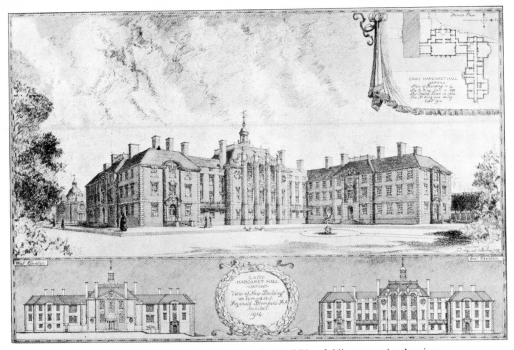

51 Lady Margaret Hall. The Wordsworth building is to the left of Blomfield's perspective drawing

52 Lady Margaret Hall, the interior of the library

53 Goldsmith's College, extensions. A perspective drawing by James B. Fulton

to give greater emphasis to certain important elements. The residential blocks are unassuming in character, but the link, or entrance, building is rather grand, with decorated pediment and a semi-dome over the door. On the first floor of this building is the library, expressed on the east elevation by three tall arched windows. Internally, this is handled in a manner reminiscent of Wren and popular with many British architects at this time: a vaulted ceiling, intersected at right angles by smaller vaults running from the arched window heads. Bookcases are built-in under the entablatures supporting the subsidiary vaults. It is a very pleasant room, efficient yet full of character.

The extension of 1926 is more severe. There is less detail and use of stone, the openings being treated very plainly. The 'Georgian' style rather than 'Wrenaissance' is in evidence. Indeed, Blomfield categorises all his buildings in the college as 'simple and modest Georgian'.

In 1929, after nearly thirty-five years' work at Lady Margaret Hall, Blomfield was replaced as architect by Giles Gilbert Scott. There was almost certainly some ill feeling over this, and the political machinations leading to Scott's appointment were unclear. In a letter to Scott written in March 1929 Blomfield says: 'So far as I am concerned you can go ahead, but don't alter my library, you will spoil it if you do.'[7]

Blomfield's extension to Goldsmith's College of 1907, which includes the provision of art and craft rooms, classrooms and other study areas, once again shows the influence of Wren, especially in the treatment of the central feature, with its round windows, separated by stone pilasters, reminiscent of Hampton

87

54 The Carrington Building, Sherborne School

55 The North Court range, with gatehouse and tower, Sherborne

56 The light-weight timber-framed gymnasium, Sherborne

Court. This style was suitable for this type of design work because repetitive elements could be easily handled, and the scale imposed by the internal activities was suitably resolved with features taken from the great houses of the seventeenth century. Earlier works, however, such as the Hammersmith Girls' School, seem rather clumsy and unrefined when compared to the later parts of Lady Margaret Hall.

There are, though, exceptions to Blomfield's developing 'Wrenaissance' manner evident in some of the extensive works undertaken for Sherborne School, and it is clear that when circumstances dictated he was prepared to forego his principles.

His first contact with Sherborne dates back to 1894, when he was commissioned to provide panelling and interior decoration to a hall built in the Gothic Revival style and known as The Big School.[8] A large proportion of the estimated cost of £590 was donated by a master, H. R. King, with the proviso that Blomfield should be employed as architect. King was a distinguished scholar and had been one of Blomfield's friends at Oxford. Nevertheless, it was another fifteen years before more substantial work was required, and in 1909 the Carrington Building was begun, comprising a number of classrooms, and linked to an old silk mill which adjoined the site. Stylistically, and despite some typical 'Wrenaissance' details, there is an odd reversion to an earlier Norman Shaw manner evident in the shaped gables located at either end of the range. The building is not highly finished, and this probably accounts for the low contract price of just under £5000.

The new buildings for North Court are even more retrogressive, and are in the Gothic style, but here Blomfield had to fit into a context with a strong existing character. A long range of building was proposed, with a right-angled return at the east side to contain the court, but the whole scheme was not completed and that part which was, was undertaken in two phases. The first was built in 1913, and its complementary half with gatehouse and tower, in 1923. Blomfield's Gothic is half-hearted and sparsely detailed, and it is interesting to note that internal features, such as architraves and door heads are classical in style.

Blomfield's work at Sherborne did not terminate here, and he was responsible for several smaller schemes, including the war memorial staircase to the chapel, an extraordinary gymnasium building of lightweight timber construction, and a modest 'Wrenaissance' music school, all built during the 1920s.

The design of educational buildings provided the opportunity for the expansion of architectural vocabulary from domestic up to large-scale buildings. As such, this segment of practice helped Blomfield to develop his version of the 'Wrenaissance' style to a scale suitable for commercial and civic works.

57 The Army and Navy Stores warehouse, Greycoat Place, Westminster, now considerably altered

Buildings for Commerce

Blomfield's major commercial buildings came after the First World War. Before 1914, however, he was involved fitfully with a few projects, of which the most outstanding were a warehouse for the Army and Navy Co-operative Society in Greycoat Place, Westminster, and the London and County Bank, King's Road, Chelsea.

The warehouse, completed by 1901, was an interesting design, now drastically altered.[9] Initially its site had been occupied by run-down tenements with irregular frontages. Blomfield evened out the building line, to produce a gently curving façade onto the street, ten bays long. The two end bays were occupied by staircases, with the storage for wine and foodstuffs on upper floors between the staircases. The middle eight bays of the ground floor comprised access to loading areas, the first floor being supported on granite Tuscan columns. Above this the building was constructed of brick, with the quoins to the piers, which separated certain bays, picked out in Portland stone. These piers were then linked by arches as they surmounted the fourth-floor level, bringing a large scale to the street. There was also a high-level projecting cornice, above which ran a row of windows with arched and circular openings. All in all the warehouse was a grand and confident piece of design.

It is difficult to pinpoint the origins of its style, but one imagines that a large and important commercial building of the late seventeenth century would have looked like this, had modern constructional techniques been available. It demonstrates an understanding of the architectural forms of that period and also of large-scale design, never quite so successfully achieved again.

58 The London and County Bank, King's Road, Chelsea

It has a lack of self-consciousness also to be noted in the rather humble garage and storage buildings in Davies Mews, London W1, which date from about the same time.

The London and County Bank, completed in 1909, is in a more conventional Blomfield 'Wrenaissance' style. The ground floor is of stone with heavily accentuated horizontal joints, and above are five rather narrow bays separated by brick pilasters. The two large arched windows that pierce the main façade at ground floor are reminiscent of those intended by Shaw for his Quadrant in Regent Street. The building is carefully detailed and executed with panache. It is solid and dignified, but lacks pomposity.[10]

Earlier, in 1900, Blomfield had attempted some very large-scale urban design by entering the ill-fated Aldwych competition. The LCC Improvements Committee invited eight architects to submit entries, but both the competition and its aims were ill-conceived and nothing was built at the time. The purpose was to provide façades for the new 'crescent' intended to join the proposed 'Kingsway' to the Strand. Blomfield's entry strangely foreshadowed his work of twenty years later: the Quadrant, Regent Street, and the Headrow, Leeds. *The Builder* said of his design:

> It has a large pilaster order, which is of stone on a brick fond . . . and is more essentially a street architecture design than most of them – a distinct attempt to combine usefulness with effect. The dominant idea in it is to have a succession of series of large arched openings in the ground storey, suitable for shop windows, interrupted at intervals by more solidly treated blocks . . . being left almost plain.[11]

59 The Public Library, Lincoln

Blomfield used his usual style but the design seems laboured, and lacks any flair. It may be that such large expanses of façade proved daunting, resulting in the use of disparate elements. Some ideas were revived in later schemes: the splayed corner treatment in the Headrow, and the notion of carrying the building over and above streets, more fully tackled in the Quadrant and the Headrow. The arched ground-floor windows are not quite as cramped as those in Shaw's design for the Quadrant which Blomfield criticised, nevertheless they are remarkably similar.

Blomfield's dislike of competitions was, no doubt, reinforced by his experience with the Aldwych fiasco, but it was a useful exercise for future years.

Public Buildings

The design of public buildings, like commercial work, did not occupy Blomfield much before 1914. What he did was diverse and interesting, though lacking in thematic consistency.

He had only two public libraries to his credit, even though this was a rapidly increasing building type in the Edwardian period. One is an early work, the library at Hertford, dating from the late 1880s which has already been mentioned. By the time he designed his second library, in Lincoln, more than twenty years later, he would undoubtedly have been embarrassed by his first effort. The Lincoln Free Library is not grand in scale, but it is grand in style. A stone-faced single-storey building with a raised central portion surmounted by a dome, decorated with swags and sculpted heads. In appearance it is quite foreign to Lincoln. Why Blomfield should have departed from his usual materials of brick with stone dressings is not clear, as it would have suited this project well. The overtones of French architecture in the design may be the result of the architect's enthusiasm for some small exquisite Continental building, or simply, perhaps, due to pressure from the client for an elaborate piece of work. Overall, this is a thorough and amusing design.

Perhaps the most unusual public building designed by Blomfield during the period is also situated in Lincoln. This is the extraordinary water tower, erected in 1910. The water tank itself is supported high up on a cylindrical brick tower, and Blomfield enclosed this with what amounts to a large stone box. The *Architects' and Builders' Journal* notes that 'the idea of a lofty keep was taken as the motive of the design'.[12] This was so that the building would be suitable for its setting and not form an unpleasant contrast with the west towers of the cathedral or the outline of the castle, an important point as the structure is positioned on the same ridge as the cathedral, and can be seen from miles away, across the flat countryside.

Blomfield built his structure from Darley stone and decorated it with iron stone, inlaid flush, forming a chequerboard pattern across the top quarter of

60 The Water Tower, Lincoln. Blomfield's drawing, 1909, exaggerates its scale

the tower. Panels are corbelled out on each side at this level, and adorned with hooded cartouches. The building is huge and rather frightening. Fortunately, it is not nearly as monstrous in real life as it appears in Blomfield's perspective drawing. Its style must owe something to the architect's interest in fortifications and massive forms, and the design reinforces rather than diminishes the ponderous bulk of the tower.

In contrast, the United University Club, Pall Mall, is one of his most celebrated buildings, a suave and sophisticated design. Unlike the other clubs with which he was involved, the whole building is his.[13] It is located in a prominent and important position near to Trafalgar Square, at the junction of Pall Mall East and Suffolk Street.

The Club was not built all at one time, but was extended on two occasions, in 1924 and 1938. These extensions conformed externally to the design of the first phase, made in 1905 and built the following year. The appearance of the building is reminiscent of French eighteenth-century architecture, particularly in its proportions and use of detail. It accords with many of Blomfield's often-voiced philosophies of architectural design, and coincided with his work on the history of French architecture, yet it is not at all typical of his contemporary style. Nevertheless, it was happily in keeping with the general liking for things French that was encouraged by the taste of the sovereign.

Financial constraints seem to have been minimised in the construction of this building, and its purpose was to provide luxurious accommodation. Indeed, the old Club was pulled down in order that a more commodious one might be built. There were six floors altogether, including the basement, the floor at roof-balustrade level and the roof storey itself. The basement accommodated the kitchen and other service areas, whilst the top three floors were given over mainly to bedrooms. Principal rooms were located on ground, first and second floors. They were very grand spaces: the smoking room and reading room, the coffee room, dining room and strangers' room, all of which could be opened into each other, the library and billiards rooms. Finishes and materials were sumptuous. Much of the woodwork was in figured Spanish mahogany and Sienna marble was used in the library. Elsewhere there was mahogany panelling, and a variety of marble wall linings were used in the entrance hall. Externally, the building was clad in Portland stone, then becoming the most acceptable external material for any building of quality in the metropolis, and the roof was covered with green Westmorland slates.

The benefits of modern technology were fully integrated into the luxurious scheme. Constructionally, a steel skeleton was used and floors were of 'fire-resisting' concrete construction. A passenger lift ran up to the third floor, and there was a double service lift from the basement kitchen to the first-floor dining room. There was electric lighting, and communications were effected by means of bells, telephones and speaking tubes. Hot-water radiators pro-

61 Cyril Farey's perspective of the United University Club, drawn at the time of the final extension in 1939

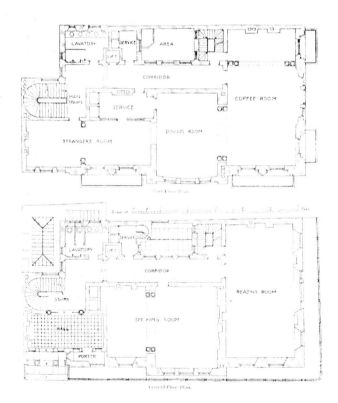

62 Ground- and first-floor plans of the United University Club, showing the extent of the first phase of building in 1906

vided central heating, but many fireplaces were installed, doubtless necessary to supplement the heating system, but also useful as focal points for after-dinner brandies.

This building is one of Blomfield's most successful works. Although a little rigid in appearance, it encapsulates in its design the world of the privileged classes in Edwardian England. It is consistent and appropriate in its architectural language, sumptuous without being vulgar.

Ecclesiastical Work

Many of Blomfield's earliest schemes were concerned with renovation, restoration and additions to small church buildings. Presumably this work derived originally from his uncle's practice, and was eventually forsaken, for though restoration was close to Blomfield's heart, Gothic architecture was not.

Beckley Church, already mentioned, is a good example of this kind of commission. It is located in a small village close to Rye and near the Burra Estates. It is possible that it was through his wife and her family that Blomfield came to know the church and eventually undertook restoration.

The building itself is mainly fourteenth century, with walling in local rubble; fairly low with big roofs, stubby tower and broached spire. Apart from general restoration, Blomfield appears to have added windows, dormers, and an extension to the south aisle. The treatment of the windows is rather curious. The one to the south aisle chapel is square headed, and divided by stone mullions into three parts, each of which contains a strange device in wrought iron. This has a plant-like form, and is very arts and crafts in feeling.

Blomfield's belief in sensitive restoration is exemplified in his work at St Peter's, Molash[14] and St George's, Ivychurch, both in Kent. The church at Molash was in a state of delapidation and Blomfield reinforced and repaired the roof and buttresses and refloored the whole building. Notable old features, such as fragments of ancient painted glass were carefully preserved or adapted. His most peculiar ecclesiastical commission, though, was the rebuilding of the St Antonien Kapelle, Berne, Switzerland, in 1891. Blomfield's perspective drawing of the scheme looks like a Dürer illustration. There is a small flèche poised on top of the building, but the main roof ends in a sort of half-hexagon form. The roof projects over the main walls, and is supported on brackets in the form of screaching and grotesque birds. Why he was tempted to produce such a strange piece of work is not certain, but it does bear some relationship to the more extreme side of arts and crafts design.

St Andrew's, Limpsfield Chart, Surrey, one of Blomfield's few original churches, also shows evidence of arts and crafts forms, but in a much more gentle way. It is wide in relation to its length, with a stumpy little tower and

63 (left) Blomfield's scheme for the rebuilding of St Antonien Kapelle, Berne

64 (above) St Andrew's Church, Limpsfield Chart, Surrey

short spire. The arches are rather 'flat' and there is a huge tiled roof. The whole is very cosy and rather quaint.[15]

Blomfield gradually dissociated himself from church architecture, but he maintained a connection with the Church of England by designing various smaller items for use within ecclesiastical buildings. The altar cross and candlesticks for All Saints' Church, Carshalton, which he and his uncle extended at the same time, were early examples. These items were executed in brass and were strongly arts and crafts in feeling, with heart motifs and thorns. They were fashionably of their time. The processional cross for St

65 Altar cross and candlesticks for Carshalton Church, Surrey, 1891

66 Memorial pulpit, Farnham Church, Surrey, 1898

Paul's Cathedral is another example of small-scale work for ecclesiastical use. Designed in 1897, it has an enamelled figure of Christ, surrounded by gilt work.

Blomfield designed several church memorials after the First World War, but some of his most interesting pieces of church furniture are pulpits. Examples are to be found at Lavant, Chichester (1895) and Farnham (1898). The Memorial Pulpit, Farnham Church, is overtly 'Wrenaissance' in style. There is no suggestion of any arts and crafts influence. The cherubs, curving balusters and panelling are all derived from Caroline precedent.

These small-scale designs show more diversity of style than the rest of Blomfield's architecture and there is a willingness to explore different idioms, though not in any very positive way. Overt arts and crafts influence, however, died with the 1890s and exuberant 'Wrenaissance' work became more staid after the turn of the century. The pattern of practice, anyway, was radically changed by the First World War, and Blomfield's later work has less *joie de vivre*, though it is often on a much larger scale.

CHAPTER 6
THE GRAND MANNER

The First World War was a watershed in Blomfield's career. Before the war he was well known to his fellow professionals and to the country gentry as a leading architect. It was after 1918, however, when his country-house practice had almost completely collapsed, that his name became familiar to the general public. The design of prestigious projects such as the buildings in the Quadrant, Regent Street, and his involvement with war memorials, from the Menin Gate down to fairly modest war crosses in provincial towns, ensured that he was mentioned in the popular press. He became a doyen of the profession, someone to look to for advice on matters of architectural taste. As one of the country's foremost 'establishment' architects he was, of course, subject to attack from the idealists of the rising generation, and he must be, for instance, one of the 'be-knighted' architects referred to in John Betjeman's *Ghastly Good Taste*. He remained a symbol of professional competence into the 1930s, however, as a distinguished practitioner upon whom local authorities and public bodies could call with assurance. All this was brought into question by a major professional blunder, which could have ruined a less self-confident man, but which he managed to survive.

Blomfield's practice, in a sense, contracted during the post-war period. Commissions were not so varied as they had been, but the scale of the works undertaken was different. Generally, buildings were much larger, though in many cases architectural details were repetitive and the value of the construction set against the amount of design work was high. Therefore, although the practice was probably profitable in the 1920s, the atmosphere must have been somewhat staid, if not actually enervating, with large jobs rumbling forward for years on end. Some of these commissions were concerned only with external appearance and the detailing of façades, rather than design of whole buildings. Also, Blomfield's son, Austin, had been taken into partnership, and it may be that much of this tedious work was put upon his shoulders. The elder Blomfield maintained and, indeed, seems to have increased, his involvment in public affairs and debate, which went on almost to his death in 1942.

The new work undertaken gave Blomfield an opportunity to practice design in the 'grand manner'. He had been enthusiastic about this for many years, but few suitable commissions came his way. He had also lost a major opportunity in the most ironic circumstances. This was the design for the great Imperial capital of India, New Delhi. His very success militated against him.

He was President of the RIBA in 1912 when the appointment of the architect for the city was to be made, and he was called upon to advise the Government of a suitable candidate. He could not, of course, put forward his own name, but had he not been President it is probable that he would have accepted

Sir Reginald Blomfield, *c.* 1919

eagerly had he been asked. He recommended Edwin Lutyens, perhaps the most talented architect to work in the new classical style, although several years junior to Blomfield. It appears that Blomfield expected to be nominated by Lutyens as associate for the project, but Lutyens eventually chose an old colleague, Herbert Baker, apparently because he felt that Blomfield would be 'too strong'. Blomfield first learned of his rejection from the newspapers, and this almost certainly led to some ill feeling between the two men, which increased with the years.[1] Later, he did not support Lutyens over the catastrophic disagreement with Baker concerning the approach to the Viceroy's house.

Blomfield's health broke down in 1914, even without the burden of Delhi, but the war eased his professional involvement. In its wake it brought work for the Imperial War Graves Commission and, following on from this, the designs of memorials and monuments for other bodies and authorities. These constituted a large proportion of his output from the end of the war up to the mid 1920s.

'Silent Cities'

The Imperial War Graves Commission was set up in 1917 with the purpose of providing graves and memorials for British and Empire soldiers who had been killed during the war. The carnage was so great that not only were there hundreds of thousands of graves to be dug, but thousands more bodies were missing altogether. The provision of cemeteries and collective memorials was therefore a mammoth task.

The newly established Commission appointed the Chief Librarian of the British Museum as adviser 'in regard to the architectural treatment and lay-out of cemeteries', but although he laid down broad lines of approach it was decided to employ architects to undertake the actual design work. Three principal architects were duly appointed of whom Reginald Blomfield was one, the others being Lutyens and Baker.[2] Their first task was to visit the temporary burial places in Northern France and Belgium to consider how they could best be made into suitable permanent cemeteries. Blomfield, Baker and Lutyens all visited Hesdin, where the War Graves Staff was located, to discuss ideas for organisation and design, and it was eventually decided that each should be allocated a specific geographical area of which they would have overall charge.

Prototype cemeteries were at first constructed and the most successful chosen to provide a model for subsequent projects.[3] Even so, some quite drastic modifications had to be made to the original idea of what was to be provided. The members of the Commission, Blomfield claims, had little or no experience of the procedure of building, or of the upsets and setbacks that

67 The full-size prototype of the War Cross, without its bronze sword

occur so often during the building process. He even had to explain to them the meaning of 'specifications' and 'quantities' and 'the ordinary methods of obtaining tenders and drawing up building contracts'.[4] They were, it seems, more than normally taken aback by costs, constructional errors, extensions in time and the artistic intransigence of architects.

Costs, more importantly, were much more than had been bargained for. They had been estimated originally on pre-war figures but by the time that construction was due to begin had risen to two or three times as much. Also the work took much longer than was expected. The Commission reacted by omitting some facilities and by cutting the size and quality of certain elements.

Each cemetery was to have two important features: a 'War Cross' designed by Blomfield and a 'Stone of Remembrance' by Lutyens. The Lutyens altar stone was sophisticated but relied for its effect upon its apparent simplicity and bulk, and could not be reduced in size or quality without loss of character and intent. Lutyens, therefore, forbade any alterations, and this led to the omission of this very expensive item from some smaller cemeteries. Blomfield, on the other hand, made himself agreeable to the Commission by suggesting various cost-saving measures and also by ensuring that his cross could be constructed in varying sizes.

The 'Cross of Sacrifice' was very carefully considered.[5] Although it was suggested that a Celtic or medieval form might do, Blomfield thought that neither was appropriate:

> What I wanted to do in designing this Cross was to make it as abstract and impersonal as I could, to free it from any association with any particular style, and, above all, to keep clear of any of the sentimentalities of Gothic. This was a man's war far too terrible for any fripperies, and I hoped to get within range of the infinite in this symbol of the ideals of those who had gone out to die.[6]

He had had experience of designing free-standing monuments earlier in his career. In 1903, for instance, he was responsible for the memorial to the South African War at his old school, Haileybury. It consisted of a stone obelisk with bronze decorative additions, surmounted by a stone ball and set upon a heavily

68 The South African War Memorial, Haileybury

scrolled podium. Three years later he designed the rather more staid Paul's Cross, which had a Doric column supporting Bertram Mackennal's figure of St Paul. It was located in St Paul's Churchyard next to the great Cathedral. The appearance of the War Cross, though, does not indicate any particular stylistic precedent. It is stark and modern, definitely of the twentieth century. Today it may seem mundane, but at the time of its introduction its austere quality must have made it quite distinctive to the general public.

Apart from its presence in all of the Imperial War Graves Commission cemeteries it became popular as a local war memorial, and was also pirated by stone masons who proceeded to produce their own versions, copying from existing examples or press photographs.

The cross itself was tall and plain, constructed in stone, and tapering towards the top. It was set upon a three tier octagonal podium, and attached to it was a large sword of bronze, 'to identify it with war'. There was some doubt as to the suitability of the design by the Commission at first because they felt that 'it reflected a Catholic rather than the Anglican tradition'.[7]

However, this doubt was soon dispelled and the cross became a feature not only of the European cemeteries, but of those in all parts of the Empire, even appearing in remote places in Africa. When the Second World War came the cross was again approved as a memorial.

69 The War Memorial, Bath, comprising cross and stone screen. Drawing by A. C. Fare, 1926

70 Design for chapel and approach, British Military Cemetery, St Sever, Rouen, 1919

The design was worked out on a proportional system using the diameter of the shaft immediately above the base as a module. Blomfield thus proposed four sizes: 14 feet, 18 feet, 20 feet and 24 feet high, with all parts scaled up or down proportionately. Some crosses were set against a stone screen upon which the names of the missing were recorded.

The austere nature of this work was carried through into the overall design of the cemeteries. Blomfield, as principal architect, had a staff of assistant architects and draughtsmen, including his son Austin, many of whom had fought in the war. They were entrusted with the designs of certain cemeteries, subject to the principal's approval. He was at great pains to see that they should not produce anything sentimental or maudlin, but should remember the huge scale of the sacrifice. He therefore wrote a memorandum headed *Advice for the use of the Junior Architects*. The design of the cemeteries, it said, should be governed by the 'fit commemoration' of those who had died and by 'the abstract expression of the idea of sacrifice and heroic death for a great cause'. Blomfield went on to describe useful precedents:

I warned them that in regard to the design of buildings they could not be too simple and even austere, and that they would do well to take as

71 Design for chapel, British Military Cemetery, Lyssenthoek

their model of inspiration the manner of Vauban, the great engineer of
Louis XIV, as shown in his forts and military stations. In regard to the
lay-out of the grounds and planting, I advised them to follow the
straight forward methods of the Formal Garden, with careful
observance of the relative value of the expanses of grass in relation to
the serried ranks of the white Portland headstones, all of which were
to a uniform design.[8]

These words seem to have been heeded, the cemeteries achieving their effect
by use of simple elements, sometimes on a very large scale. They possess
a degree of calm with their long straight vistas and restrained use of incident.
Broad, smooth, grassy avenues lined with row upon row of simple white headstones succeed where a more romantic or small-scale approach would probably have failed. It is, perhaps, ironic that one of Blomfield's few chances
for a complete and overall use of the 'grand manner' should have been in
providing graves and memorials for the dead.

Memorials and Monuments

Despite the fact that the War Cross was plagiarised, Blomfield was often called in to design local memorials.[9] At the same time, there were certain private commissions for memorials to individuals, usually taking the form of wall monuments inside existing buildings. Major opportunities came with proposals for two important works in London: the Belgian War Memorial and the RAF Memorial, both of which were to be located on the Thames Embankment.

The Belgian Memorial, presented to the British Nation 'from the grateful people of Belgium', consists of a sculpture by Victor Rousseau, behind which is a hemicycle of Portland stone. Severely classical, this now forms a little enclosure to one side of the major road running along the Embankment. Although grand in conception it is a tiny static space compared to the huge river of traffic adjacent. Ironically, a pedestrian crossing now leads across the asphalt on the centre line of the whole composition. Blomfield received the Order of Leopold I from the King of the Belgians for this work, but its setting is incongruous and detrimental to the design intention.

The RAF Memorial is a somewhat happier concept, based on the 'pylon' motif also used for war memorials at Luton and Torquay. The site, on the landing of one of the river staircases, was constricted, and Blomfield had to bear in mind how area might be related to height without injuring the proportions. The monument was surmounted by a gilded globe, with a golden eagle rising from it, thus increasing its effective height. The design of the pylon is not particularly inspired, and it is the eagle that catches the imagination, yet overall it provides an effective and distinctive urban incident.

72 The Belgian War Memorial, London

73 Model of the RAF Memorial, with the eagle facing away from the river

One senses a certain unease in Blomfield's urban memorials. Perhaps his approach was dependent to a large extent upon control of the surroundings. This was not really possible in most locations, but in the case of his most famous work of this type, the Menin Gate, he was able to exercise choice in terms of site.

The Menin Gate is the largest and most celebrated memorial that Blomfield designed, but it probably owes its fame to its size, position and significance rather than to architectural quality. This is not to say that it is an unsuccessful design. Charles Reilly referred to it as a concept 'far-reaching in its range and unfaltering in its purpose, rising superior to all entanglements of detail'.[10] In other words, it exemplified Blomfield's philosophy of architecture, largely as formulated before the war, but most clearly put into practice after 1918.

Blomfield first became involved with the project at Ypres in 1919. He was sent out by the War Office to report on suitable sites for a memorial to commemorate 'all those who had died in the war on the Ypres salient and had no known graves'.[11]

He chose the Menin Gate site where, to the east of Ypres, the road passed through the old fortifications which Vauban had erected in the seventeenth century. It was the route taken by British soldiers on their way to the German lines, and thus of great significance. Fortunately it was also a site with great architectural capabilities. There were ramparts, a moat and causeway. Opportunities thus existed for the reflection of the building in the water of the moat and for creating an important piece of townscape at a significant nodal point. The choice of the site, therefore, was a very important factor in the success of the project.

74 The RAF Memorial, the Embankment, London

75 The Prince of Wales at the unveiling of the RAF Memorial, 1923.
Blomfield is second from right, partially obscured

76 The Menin Gate, looking across the 'moat'

Blomfield went on to think about the form that the building itself would take. Apart from its symbolic nature it had a functional purpose, which was to display of the names of over 60,000 dead. The building was to be a record, a symbol and a large element of urban design. The design which resulted clearly contained references to Roman civic architecture but the detailed concept was based, so Blomfield records in his *Memoirs*, on the seventeenth-century fortifications at Nancy.[12] Here, an elliptical brick tunnel ran over a roadway, lit by openings in the crown of the vault. This idea was translated into a Hall of Memory, some 115 feet long by 66 feet wide, which was constructed in reinforced concrete, coffered on its underside. The vault spanned the road and the footpaths to either side and was lined with 1,200 stone panels recording the names of the dead. Staircases ran from both sides of the Hall up to the adjoining ramparts.

Externally, the Gate consists of a monumental arch at each end, flanked by twin Doric columns, of enormous height, carrying entablatures. A pedestal rises above each arch, supporting sculpture. The long sides of the building have loggias with Doric colonnades and are terminated by pavilions. The whole structure, externally, is composed of brick and Euville stone.

The history of the construction of the Menin Gate, however, is not a happy one. Blomfield had been commissioned to examine sites as early as 1919, but after submission of this report little was done and it was not until the Imperial War Graves Commission took the initiative in 1922 that he was able to begin work. His working drawings and specifications were completed by June of that year. The early delay, though, established a pattern of difficulties and holdups that was to be repeated throughout the construction of the Gate.

The first main problem was with the foundations, where running sand had to be coped with. Sir Maurice Fitzmaurice, an engineer, was consulted and suggested that the building should be supported by a 30 foot thick concrete raft, laid across the whole expanse of the site. Blomfield wisely ignored this

77 Interior of the Menin Gate, showing tablets of stone recording the names of the missing

advice and, working with Oscar Faber, produced a scheme with a two-foot-thick reinforced-concrete raft supported on reinforced-concrete piles.[13]

Problems of time and money also beset the building of the Menin Gate and Blomfield states that although the contractors were excellent and the work well executed, by the time the Gate was completed the project was no less than two years behind schedule.[14] Even so, there was a further delay and the official opening ceremony did not occur until 1927.

The building, when completed, was lacking in one respect: it could only contain 57,000 names, and so the missing names were transferred to another memorial. A further disappointment to Blomfield was that he had hoped to make a more effective urban design by keeping back the building lines of the devastated town of Ypres so that a visual link could be established between the Cloth Hall and the Menin Gate. He also wanted to form a 'place' (French: *place*) on the far side of the moat and the causeway. This would have helped to expand the urban scale. The citizens of Ypres would have none of this, though, and insisted on building to existing lines, thereby reducing the impact of Blomfield's work and robbing him yet again of a chance to produce a satisfactory design in the grand urban manner.

The Menin Gate earned for Blomfield the 'Order of the Crown of Belgium'. The reception from other sources was mixed, however. *The Times* said that the Gate was of 'that austere beauty which befits the grand but cruel memories which it recalls'. Others were not so kind, and one malicious critic noted that it was 'made up from the stock of architectural commonplaces . . . bereft of the enthusiasm and patience which should endow it with the impress of life, lacking power and significance, missing utterly the quality which would prove it has been played over in every part by the sensibility of human intelligence and emotion'.[15]

Blomfield, though, was more generous to his own creation, quoting at length in his *Memoirs* from the rather inaccurate and high-flown description written by Stephan Zweig for the *Berliner Tagblatt* in September 1928, in which he says that 'Ypres has gained a new monument, and – let me say at once – one that is both spiritually and artistically, profoundly impressive.'[16]

Blomfield also says that of all his buildings the Menin Gate is the only one that he would not wish to change. 'If I am ever remembered', he wrote, 'I hope it may be by the Menin Gate, my design for the completion of the Quadrant and Lambeth Bridge'.[17]

The Quadrant

This scheme for one of the most important streets in London was a very prestigious commission for Blomfield. There were many constraints upon the design, however, and he had anything but a fresh start upon this project which had a long, chequered and rather sad history.

John Nash was the original architect of Regent Street. He submitted a scheme to the Department of Woods and Forests for the new thoroughfare in 1810, which was eventually undertaken and completed, as far as Piccadilly, by about 1825. A fine piece of urban design, consistent in scale and detail, one of its most outstanding features was a magnificent quadrant which swung it east to make the junction with Piccadilly.

The street became very popular during the nineteenth century and the shops were well patronised by the aristocracy and gentry. Towards the end of the century, however, shopping patterns changed. The street began to cater for the expanding middle classes, profit margins were cut and the turnover of stock increased. This led to the need for extra storage space, and the increase in size of shop units. Two or three shops were often knocked together and storage facilities increased by using first-floor accommodation and by extending to the rear. Nash's relatively small-scale brick and stucco buildings could not withstand such developments, and by the 1890s it was noted that their structural stability which had never been good had been affected for the worse by alterations, in some cases giving rise to dangerous conditions.[18]

It was quite obvious, therefore, that demolition and rebuilding at a scale suitable for modern shopping would have to take place. Meanwhile, plans were going ahead for a new hotel, one façade of which would impinge upon Piccadilly, and the other on the Quadrant. The Commissioner of Woods and Forests set up an advisory committee, which appointed Richard Norman Shaw to design the exterior of the hotel and the shops beneath. Starting in 1905, Blomfield records that Shaw 'prepared a grandiose design [for the Quadrant], with rusticated arches on the ground floor, and rusticated Ionic columns above, running through three storeys and supporting a bold entablature. Above this was a row of stone dormers and an immense slate roof with dormers, and lofty stone chimney stacks at frequent intervals.'[19]

At the same time Shaw put forward a proposal for the rearrangement of Piccadilly Circus. The Quadrant would sweep round and emerge into a new square some 300 feet long and 200 feet wide, akin to a French 'place'. The Shaftesbury Memorial was to form a centrepiece, but this plan was rejected by the LCC in 1906 on the grounds of excessive cost.[20]

The hotel was completed in 1908, by which time the company which financed it was bankrupt. To make matters worse, the shopkeepers of the Quadrant were unhappy about the cost and practicality of Shaw's design. This opposition prevented Shaw's scheme from being adopted for the whole Quadrant. An attempt was made by the Department of Woods and Forests, through the architect Henry Tanner, to modify the design, but Shaw would not countenance alterations, and with much bitterness and disappointment he resigned. He wrote, pathetically: 'I have pored over the design for the Quadrant till I am worn out. . .' Shaw stopped work early in 1912 and died later that year.[21]

The Commissioner of Woods and Forests now appointed a new committee to look at the Quadrant, and Blomfield was included by virtue of his position as President of the RIBA. The committee reported in 1913, but although

78 A contemporary drawing showing the Quadrant from Piccadilly Circus

79 The Quadrant looking towards Piccadilly Circus. Norman Shaw's work
is indicated by the position of the great chimneys

80 The arch over Air Street

it recommended that the general style and character of the building was to follow that of Shaw's hotel, with the offending arcades and the giant Ionic columns omitted, it was superseded by a third committee in 1915 before any action was taken. Blomfield suggested that Sir Aston Webb and Ernest Newton, now President of the RIBA, should sit with him on this committee. As a result of their deliberations, they presented a report saying that any new scheme should 'alter Shaw's design without destroying it', and recommending 'that the main lines of his entablature, the dormers and the roof lines should be maintained, but the chimney stacks omitted'.[22]

The Commissioner of Woods and Forests then asked Webb, Newton and Blomfield to produce a fresh design. What happened next is described by Blomfield. 'As it was impossible for three architects of widely differing views to make the design, and I had been connected with the affair from the first, I was asked by Webb and Newton to undertake the design.'[23]

This may be a simplified and euphemistic account of what happened, but at any rate by 1916 Blomfield was already at work and had resolved the design in some detail. The overall scheme and details were ready by 1917 and, in fact, Webb, Newton and Blomfield signed the drawings of the elevations to the north and south sides of the Quadrant in 1917, even though, as Blomfield tells us, 'Webb and Newton did not see the drawings till they were signed by us'.[24] In 1918 Blomfield also designed the buildings at the top of Lower Regent Street, that is, the south-east and south-west corners of Piccadilly Circus. So, all in all, Blomfield's work included 'the whole of the Quadrant (except the Piccadilly Hotel) the County Fire Office, the return façade in Piccadilly up to the Hotel, and the buildings at the top of Lower Regent Street on both sides of the Street'.[25]

In his designs, Blomfield had maintained the basic lines of Shaw's early scheme but his work was very different in character, even considering that he was to follow the principles laid down by the 1913 and 1915 committees for the simplification of the original. Blomfield admits: 'The curious thing is that though I had every intention of being loyal to Shaw's design, by the time I had got round the corner into Piccadilly, the design had completely changed its character.[26]

Blomfield had not had a very favourable impression of Shaw's scheme from the start, and found it was a strange mixture of design in the 'grand manner' and 'of that free and fanciful invention of which Shaw was a consummate master'. Blomfield's response to the problem was more bland and urbane. Its inspiration was rooted in eighteenth-century French urban design, and in the *Memoirs* he explains that his solution of the problem 'was to treat Shaw's building as the centre of one great composition . . . with plain curtain façades east and west of the hotel, and pavilions at either end'. A difficulty was posed by the archway over Air Street, which Shaw had intended, but where his Ionic columns gave the impression of crushing the haunches of the arch.

81 Blomfield's scheme for remodelling Piccadilly Circus, drawn by Cyril Farey

Blomfield solved this by using a pedestal course with Roman Doric columns: 'though it was a dangerous venture to introduce two different orders under one entablature, I came to the conclusion that the whole design was so unorthodox that it really did not matter'.[27]

The buildings were constructed primarily of steel frames, with façades in Portland stone. Blomfield was responsible, though, only for the elevations and other architects had to plan interiors within his scheme. Some of these men were very distinguished in their own right. J. J. Joass, for instance, was architect for the Swan & Edgar store, which terminates the composition and takes it round the corner into Piccadilly, and Ernest Newton for the County Fire Office, which has, according to Shaw, 'the finest site in London'. Westwood and Emberton, and Henry Tanner, were also involved.

The new Quadrant, and its Piccadilly Circus adjunct, was eventually completed in 1927 and opened by King George V in June of that year. Building had not been begun until 1923, but work seems to have progressed smoothly. Reaction to the new scheme was mixed. The popular press and the shopkeepers seemed happy enough, saying that the street was suited to the spirit of the modern age. Architectural critics were harder, particularly those a generation younger than Blomfield. A. Trystan Edwards, for example, an erstwhile pupil of Blomfield, championed the old Regent Street and the fine work of Nash. He talked of the new 'heavy, forbidding, gargantuan style of architecture' and said that 'the Quadrant will be transformed into a bleak, ill-proportioned channel of practically square section, which has already in antici-

pation been compared to a drain-pipe'.[28] *The Builder* was no more kind, saying that 'the architect must look upon it [the Quadrant] with much disappointment' and noting that the 'right scale of the street [has been] destroyed'.[29]

Blomfield, however, did not regret the removal of the Nash buildings. His opinion of Nash was very low:

> When they were destroyed it became the fashion to say that they were refined and elegant buildings, showing a grace denied to what was to succeed them. When I was a student, I was taught to regard them as the last word in vulgarity and ridiculous building. In actual fact the details of the design were exceedingly trivial, and the only real merit in Nash's design was the curve of the Quadrant and a certain pleasant urbanity.[30]

Architects of Blomfield's generation were used to very high standards of building construction, and Nash's cheap and superficial stucco architecture was anathema to those with an arts and crafts background. A younger generation, represented by Trystan Edwards, criticised this attitude, accusing the older men of insensitivity towards Nash's work through their adhesion to a Victorian attitude of 'morality' in building construction. This is ironic, as Blomfield felt that he had helped to lead architecture away from the Gothic Revival and its heritage towards civilized and urbane classical design.[31]

Despite the criticism, Blomfield, as a practitioner in the 'grand manner', wished to continue his design and extend it so that it took in the whole of Piccadilly Circus. The Circus was visually disorganised, and some thought it exceedingly vulgar, with its diversity of giant illuminated advertisements. Thus, he followed in the footsteps of both Shaw and Murray, and in 1929 produced a design for the redevelopment of the whole of the Circus. As with the Shaw scheme, this was to be 'squared-off' and turned into a 'place'.[32] The style of the building followed that of the Quadrant: the block to replace the London Pavilion was to mirror the Swan & Edgar building opposite, the tall first-floor windows staring blankly at each other across the intervening 'place'. The end of Glasshouse Street was to be flanked by the County Fire Office with an identical domed block opposite. The overall effect was to provide a grand urban space in keeping with the capital city of the Empire.

It was, of course, never built. After Blomfield had finished the scheme he discovered that some of the LCC leases on land to the east of Glasshouse Street were to run until 1962. He had initially thought that they had only 15 years to run, but even so it is clear that from the outset he was looking well into the future and beyond his lifespan. He suggested that the LCC retain his plan so that it might be used when the opportunity to rebuild came along, but the council declined to do so, and the Circus remains to this day incomplete in terms of unified design.[33]

Blomfield's work on the Quadrant and the attendant publicity undoubtedly suggested his name to any provincial authority contemplating grand urban improvements. One of these was Leeds.

Urban Design in Yorkshire

In Leeds there had been thoughts about urban improvements for some time. In 1924, just after the work on the Quadrant began, a proposal was put forward by the City Council's Improvements Committee to create a great street to run from Victoria Square, in the west, down towards Quarry Hill, in the east. The new thoroughfare would incorporate Upperhead Row and Lowerhead Row, and replace existing shopping areas. No doubt civic pride and an element of competition with other large municipalities entered into the thinking behind this project. Perhaps, also, it was intended as a symbol that the city had moved into the twentieth century, and that the mean little buildings spawned by the Industrial Revolution were to be swept away and replaced by the product of a wealthy and powerful, yet enlightened authority. The street was to be 80 feet wide and 1,000 yards long, and its name, The Headrow, was decided by the public in a competition organised by the *Yorkshire Evening Post*.

Leeds did not employ a City Architect at that time, and the city engineer was responsible for all building works. It was felt, however, that an architect should be used for this special project. There was some initial wrangling, and although it was thought desirable that a local man should be chosen no agreement was reached. Thus it was decided that an impartial assessor should make the choice. Blomfield, who had acted for Leeds Corporation previously and whose name was synonymous with large-scale urban schemes, was asked to judge.[34] He came to the conclusion that a project of such magnitude could not be entrusted to a provincial architect, but should be given to someone with skill and experience in these matters. The position now seemed perfectly clear, and Blomfield himself was appointed in December 1925, 'to prepare designs, including complete working drawings, of the elevations of the buildings which may be erected to the new street'.[35]

Progress was rapid, for early in 1926 *The Builder* announced that 'Leeds Corporation last week gave formal sanction to Sir Reginald Blomfield's design'. This, of course, consisted only of the outer skin of the buildings, and other architects, such as G. W. Atkinson, were brought in to turn them into three-dimensional reality. Blomfield's job was to co-ordinate external appearance, and some contemporary publicity notes that 'the whole of the buildings on the North side of the street have to conform to a uniform design. . . . This has the effect of producing a thoroughfare of dignity and nobility probably unsurpassed in any provincial city.'[36]

The façades, apart from the shopfronts which had bronze glazing bars and fascias, were executed in red brick with Portland stone dressings and Portland stone to the ground floor. This was Blomfield's preferred combination of

82 The Headrow, Leeds, looking east from the corner of Cookridge Street

83 The Headrow, a detail as perceived by the pedestrian

84 The Headrow, an opening in the façade

materials, which he would have liked for the Quadrant. He maintained that in combination brick and stone were indigenous London materials, whereas stone by itself was not. The same could hardly have been said about Leeds, however, but red brick and white stone were used nevertheless.

The Headrow rises to a summit about one third of the way along its length from its western end, and Blomfield's blocks ascend awkwardly from either direction. At significant points, such as changes of level, major entrances, access roads and corners, which are splayed, there are 'pavilions' with Doric stone pilasters rising through the upper storeys of brick and terminating in urns. On the whole, though, decoration is kept to a minimum, even when compared to the Quadrant. The upper floors consist of plain brickwork punctuated by rectangular windows with steel casements. The ground floor is of Portland stone with deeply incised joints and round-headed openings. Blomfield used a device from Regent Street at the point where a service road pierces the façade – a stone arch, surmounted above first-floor level by a pair of Doric columns carrying the architrave and cornice to the roof parapet.

The effect is disappointing. Here was an opportunity to produce some first-rate design in the 'grand-manner', but it seems to have been lost. The design lacks wit, imagination, sparkle and originality. Indeed, some of the details appear to go back to the Aldwych competition entry of 1900. It speaks in southern accents, containing nothing of the grittiness of Leeds and its surroundings.

Blomfield continued to work on schemes associated with the Headrow during the last decade of his practice. He produced a design for the new Lewis's store in 1930, although this was not built as proposed, whilst Barclays Bank, at the junction with Vicar Lane, his only work on the south side of the steet, was completed in 1936. In addition there is a *rond-point* at the extreme eastern end, which found use as a petrol filling station. It provides a pleasant touch of consistency and it is here that the scheme's rather limited success lies. The scale and consistency of design add much to the fabric of Leeds and help to give it an urban quality previously lacking.

There was, of course, criticism of the design in local architectural circles. Some of this may have been based on envy, but it must be remembered that during the 1930s Blomfield's architecture was beginning to look very old-fashioned. Speaking to the West Yorkshire Society of Architects in 1932, its President, B. R. Gribbon, said:

Taking what has been done as a whole the effect is good, if a little inert. It is an excellent example of English Renaissance treatment, courtly as Sir Roger de Coverley, but, after all, it is a shopping street, and I do not think many firms today would appoint Sir Roger, fine gentleman though he was, as their commercial representative.[37]

85 *Rond-point* at the eastern end of the Headrow-Eastgate development

A similar criticism was eventually levelled at Ferensway in Hull. Blomfield was not commissioned to design this new thoroughfare, but was appointed assessor for the competition to select an architect. The idea of linking Paragon Square, opposite Hull's main railway station, with Beverley Road had originated before the war, but it was not until 1924, as with the Headrow, that Parliamentary powers were granted for construction. The new street was to cut through the mean development that had taken place during the city's rapid expansion in the nineteenth century. Blomfield, writing in *The Municipal Journal*, made reference to the need for change, noting that 'the streets of old cities, especially cities that have prospered, are like the old clothes of thrifty persons. They become too small, too shabby and unsuitable for further use, and it has nearly always happened that the owners have tried to bring them up to date by patchwork.'[38] Here was an attempt, however, to provide a co-ordinated and appropriate architectural design. The new street was to be 1500 feet long and 100 feet wide from face to face. As with the Quadrant and the Headrow, the design was to be only for a façade, with which individual developments along the street would be expected to conform. The function of the street was mainly to provide shopping at pavement level, with three storeys of office accommodation above, though provision was also made for a new hotel.

Prudent competitors obviously paid attention to the tastes of the assessor, and it is not surprising that the schemes placed first, second and third are very Blomfieldian in character. The winning design, by Messrs Scarlett and Ashworth, is described in Blomfield's report. It is, he writes,

> a well-proportioned, straight-forward design in brick and stone, admirably suited for its purpose. The competitor has succeeded in finding a very good proportion within the limited height of the front allowed (50 feet) and his suggestion of early eighteenth century English architecture is, in my opinion, a right treatment of the new front.[39]

The Municipal Journal, much impressed by 'the distinguished architect who acted as assessor, Sir Reginald Blomfield, RA, Litt D, FSA, Commissioner of Fine Arts of England', may have enthused about 'landmarks in the history of municipal architecture' and 'English beauty in dignity and design', but the *Architect and Building News* was less complimentary:

> The influence of Regent Street is noticeable in almost all designs sent in, being particularly so in such details as the linking archways over side roads. The selected designs cannot be said to contribute much that is an advance on their prototype, all three following accepted notions in arrangement and character. It seems possible that Regent Street may set a fashion in new streets for provincial towns, which, while all very well for the towns concerned, does not provide any new thought on what is, after all, a changing problem. . . . The mere repetition of a set of forms based on fixed ideas, however good the forms or ideas may be, is stagnation, not progress.[40]

Such comments reflect the growing disillusionment in professional circles with the type of urban design that was championed by Blomfield.

Smaller Commissions

Blomfield undertook a number of important commissions during this period apart from large-scale civic projects. Representative are three schemes which involved a range of problems, including a difficult piece of restoration, the design of a large commercial building and the design of a significant public building.

The restoration work concerned the Carlton Club, originally designed by Smirke in the manner of an Italian *palazzo*. It had been constructed with Caen stone which had 'failed completely' and in 1923 Blomfield was called in to reface the building. For both aesthetic and financial reasons he decided

DESIGN·FOR·THE·REFACING·OF·THE·CARLTON·CLUB·IN·PORTLAND·STONE· 1923 Reginald Blomfield R.A. Archt.

86 Design for refacing the Carlton Club in Portland stone

that it was necessary to redesign the elevations. This commission, by its very nature, cannot have been easy, and the position and fixing of every stone had to be decided. Furthermore, the building had not been constructed to twentieth-century standards, and it was discovered, for instance, that in the 'symmetrical' north elevation the three bays to the west of the centre projection were actually wider than those to the east. Nevertheless, the work was successfully tackled, despite a skirmish between Blomfield and Lord Curzon, who did not like the new appearance of the Club. Indeed, the result was extraordinary, as the original nineteenth-century proportions were still readable through Blomfield's severe twentieth-century classicism. There was little evidence of the 'Wrenaissance' here, and a sterile and austere Beaux-Arts manner prevailed.[41]

The new store for John Barker & Co., in Kensington High Street, completed in 1926, was designed in conjunction with H. L. Cabuche, who was employed by Barker's to plan the interior.[42] Blomfield was 'architect for the elevations'. As the building was located on a Crown site it may have been stipulated that a distinguished practitioner should be employed to design the exterior, or perhaps the company used him for reasons of prestige. There is no other explanation as to why the design should have been undertaken in this way. The store was virtually free-standing, not part of a great urban scheme as were the shops in the Quadrant.

87 Cyril Farey's drawing of John Barker's Store, Kensington, 1925

The result was far from satisfactory and, unfortunately, combined vulgarity with severity and aloofness. Neither Blomfield's beautiful sketch of the cupola nor Cyril Farey's wonderfully accomplished perspective drawing can disguise the true nature of this building. Gone is Blomfield's 'Wrenaissance' charm, in its place is an elephantine Beaux-Arts style. The apologetic sculpture and classical detail are insignificant beside the great rectangular pilasters, starting above ground floor level and shooting up through three large shopping floors. It displays the same kind of ineptitude later demonstrated at Carlton Gardens and in the proposal for Carlton House Terrace.

The Usher Art Gallery at Lincoln is, however, a different matter. It was designed at the same time as the Barker Store, and completed in 1927. It proved to be a much more manageable size. Its purpose is to house a bequest of paintings, clocks and other *objets d'art* left to the City of Lincoln by a prominent citizen, James Usher.[43]

It is a simply planned, two-storey building, with central vestibule and stairs, and galleries off to each side. Externally, and in plan form, it reads as a Beaux-Arts exercise, rather like a contemporary project at one of the thriving full-time schools of architecture. There is a Doric pilaster order, red brick panels and a central pediment over the entrance door. The building is very thoroughly designed, including the fixed furniture inside, and it has some delightful details such as the round window high up above the stairs through which

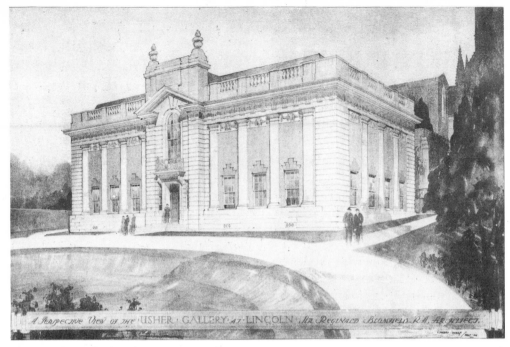

88 The Usher Gallery, Lincoln, drawn by Gordon Holt, 1926

there is a perfectly framed view of the Cathedral tower.

This extremely civilised little building is one of Blomfield's most successful late designs. His approach works well on a small and limited structure of this type. The architectural language used, though, is too cramped and restrictive for the majority of twentieth-century projects. It seems, in retrospect, that his preferred design technique was becoming obsolete and inappropriate as a response to modern problems.

CHAPTER 7
CAUSES AND COMMITTEES

Throughout the 1920s and 1930s, and despite the fact that he was well over sixty years of age by the time the war ended, Blomfield continued to participate in the work of public, official and semi-official bodies. Typical was his membership of the Royal Fine Art Commission, which was established in 1923. The foundation of this body was laid before the First World War with a proposal for a Ministry of Fine Arts. Blomfield, as President of the RIBA, had been involved, but the idea came to nothing. Perhaps it was a too grand and un-English notion for the time. The Royal Fine Art Commission itself developed from a series of conferences held by the Royal Academy in 1922 and 1923. Distinguished architects and artists made up its number, and Blomfield was involved from the beginning. The function of the Commission, to advise on matters of taste, appealed much to Blomfield, the artist-architect. He regretted that it could only operate in an advisory capacity, and he felt that its decisions were only taken into account when they fitted in with those of the Government. Membership of such a commission, however, helped to re-inforce Blomfield's position as an arbiter of taste, although there were to be some embarrassing consequences, as will be seen.

The Royal Academy

His rôle at the Royal Academy was expanded in the 1920s and 1930s and he found himself involved in many of the committees which were set up by the Academy. For instance, he was a member of the Memorials Committee, established in 1917. Besides Blomfield, the Committee consisted of painters and sculptors, including Hamo Thornycroft, with whom Blomfield had worked on previous occasions. Its outcome was a memorandum of advice on war memorials for the guidance of 'municipal and other bodies'. It was drafted by Blomfield but, as he states sourly in the *Memoirs*, 'little came of it'.

This seems to have been the way with many of the Academy's activities, and the indecisive manner in which problems were handled was particularly emphasised in the case of the Chantrey Bequest. In his will, Sir Francis Chantrey had bequeathed a fund for the purchase of works of art, and paintings had been bought from 1877 onwards. However, from the turn of the century, there had been disquiet as to how the money was spent, and a House of Lords Select Committee of 1904 had implied that the Academicians tended to buy their own works to far too great an extent. The Academy refuted this suggestion, but bickering went on for many years, not least with the Trustees of the Tate Gallery, which had responsibility for the display of what was meant to be a national collection of first-rate modern work. In May 1917 Blomfield wrote a report summing up the whole business and, finally, suggested ways of resolving the matter. This was achieved, but not until 1922, and he was shown to have been instrumental in helping with a thorny problem.[1]

The following year he produced a paper entitled 'Considerations of the Policy and Position of the Royal Academy', a document setting out various constitutional reforms. The paper was well received, and in July 1918 a constitution committee was formed to look into Blomfield's proposals. This panel made several recommendations, most of which were to do with membership of the Academy. The net result was to remove old and entrenched members, to introduce new ideas, a wider variety of people, and to give Associates better representation.

There was some difficulty in obtaining acceptance for these measures, but at last approval was given, with the added bonus that a new regulation was instituted saying that at any one time there should be at least four architect and four sculptor Academicians and Associates.

The reform had been brought about largely through Blomfield's initiative and he must have stood out as a man of considerable energy and ability among the other Academy members. He was proposed for office of President when Aston Webb, who had taken up the position in 1919, retired in 1924. His opponent was the painter Frank Dicksee. Blomfield lost the election by fourteen votes to seventeen, though had it not been for the fact that he was following the Presidency of another architect, he may well have achieved his ambition and become President of both the RA and the RIBA during his career.

More Books

His literary efforts continued unabated throughout the 1920s and 1930s, and the period was opened by the completion of one of his greatest achievements, *A History of French Architecture*.[2] This work, which traces developments between the end of the fifteenth century and the death of Louis XV, would need many pages of appraisal if it were to be examined in detail, yet its means of expression does not differ significantly from what has gone before, even though the content is new.

The writing of the book occupied Blomfield for several years, and it was published in four volumes, the first two of which appeared in 1911, and the others in 1921. Its roots go back further, however, and some of the essays included in *Studies in Architecture*, published in 1905, concern aspects of French Renaissance design. Also the excellent *Architectural Drawing and Draughtsmen*, of 1912, has a chapter on French draughtsmen of the seventeenth century. Blomfield had visited France frequently, sometimes on holiday with his family, from 1897 onwards. He collected material as he travelled, and topographical drawings may be seen in his contemporary sketch books. The length of time taken to research and write the work indicates the magnitude of the task, and this is mentioned in the introduction of Vol. 1:

> Apart from personal difficulties of time and opportunity, the subject is so vast and intricate, the material is so abundant, that there is a constant danger of losing the clue to the main track of history. . . . I have for several years endeavoured to quarter the ground in France and to study on the spot the buildings referred to in the text.[3]

The travels and 'quarterings of the ground' produced many fine sketches which act, together with photographs and contemporary drawings, as illustrations for Volumes 1 and 2. Volumes 3 and 4 are illustrated by contemporary seventeenth- and eighteenth-century engravings, some of which he discovered at Mellerstain during his work there.

This investigation of French architecture goes hand in hand with an increasing maturity and restraint to be noted in Blomfield's design work, and although overt French stylistic influence is not often present in his architecture it is clear that its philosophy and approach were studied and absorbed.

The material is written with a broad historical perspective mixed with a leavening and pertinent amount of detail which includes personal information about architects involved: 'De l'Orme died on a Sunday evening, 8th January, 1570, in his Canon's house of Notre Dame'; patrons; the background against which buildings were conceived and built, and notes on such topics as constructional systems. Blomfield's usual habit of drawing lessons from the past is here too, though related to French Renaissance examples: 'Blondel concludes his criticism with words which ought to be put up in every school of architecture, "simplicity of form, economy of ornament, reserve in the breaks ought to be held a higher beauty than any detail that invention and genius can suggest".' There is criticism, also, of contemporary historical comment about French Renaissance architecture: 'Jean Bullant has been described by that accomplished historian, M. Lemonnier, as "*un de l'Orme un peu ammoindri*". I cannot imagine any criticism much wider of the mark.' The work of the period itself does not escape, however: 'I have devoted myself in this chapter to the somewhat ungrateful task of iconoclasm, and have endeavoured to represent the master builders . . . in the sober dress of history.'[4]

These comments are supplemented by some observations on his approach to architectural history which may seem especially relevant today. 'The history of architecture has suffered from the insatiable instinct for classification', he wrote. 'History is not so easy, nor is it so accommodating to the man with a passion for system.'[5]

Nowhere does Blomfield allow 'a passion for a system' to override his consideration of the 'personal equation' of the architect when dealing with history. *Six Architects*, published in 1935, exemplifies this, as does his monograph, *Sébastien Le Prestre de Vauban*, which describes the life and work of the great seventeenth-century military engineer in some detail.[6] It is mainly drawn from French sources, but the author had a personal acquaintance with many of Vauban's works, the monumental nature of which greatly appealed to him. In his preface he expresses surprise that no English author had written about Vauban, 'one of the few honest men in the service of Louis XIV'.

The Touchstone of Architecture, published in 1925, departs from biographical matters, and is a collection of lectures and addresses delivered between 1912 and 1924. Some of these were given on momentous occasions, for example, the speech made at the presentation of the RIBA Gold Medal in 1913, others at less significant times. Generally, the themes are familiar and denounce the loss of direction in architecture and the overwhelming desire for originality at any cost. 'Atavism in Art', however, contains some rather suspect theorising about race and architectural development in Europe.

Byways – Leaves from an Architect's Note Book, which dates from 1929, is more relaxed and is the result of years of travel around Europe, being mainly concerned with France, Austria and Bavaria. It does not claim to be exhaustive, but is intended for light reading, and discusses the interrelationship between people, places and buildings. There is, for instance, in the section devoted to Vienna, a description of Casanova's adventures in the Archbishop's Palace, as well as a delineation of the palace itself.

Such a variety of literary and historic endeavour was, of course, essential to Blomfield's character, and related to this was the rôle of critical spectator and advisor, which increased after the First World War and accounts for much of his involvement in public life.

His activities show a reforming spirit, but this is oddly set against his overall conservatism. It may be said that by nature Blomfield was radical and always ready to stir up the 'establishment', but by background and intellect he was conservative.

The City Churches

The churches of the City of London, many of which were designed by Wren or his contemporaries, were found to be too great in number for the diminished population of what was essentially a business district by the early years of this century. The Assembly of the Church of England wished to demolish these redundant buildings and to sell their, by now, valuable sites for commercial development. A Commission was set up in 1919 to decide what should be done. It recommended that nineteen churches should be demolished, of which no less than thirteen were the work of Christopher Wren, and the others were by such distinguished architects as Dance and Hawksmoor. Wren's work, of course, was specially close to Blomfield's heart and he was appalled at the suggestion of the Commission, as were many others. A conference of interested parties, which included the RIBA and the Society for the Protection of Ancient Buildings, was held at the Royal Academy in 1920, when it was decided to oppose the Church's attempt to bring in an Act enabling them to destroy the City churches. A memorial of protest was sent to the Bishop of London, and Blomfield acted as the liaison man between the Conference and the Church Assembly. After much correspondence it was found that the Church Assembly would not be swayed and intended to proceed with the measure that would enable it to begin its destructive work. Blomfield, therefore, brought the matter out into the open in November 1924 with a letter to *The Times* in support of which that newspaper also published a leading article.[7] Other letters followed and public opinion moved towards the side of the parties contributing to the Academy Conference, which was held again in February 1925, the Corporation of the City of London joining in to condemn the actions of the Church Assembly. When therefore the 'Union of Benefices and Disposal of Churches (Metropolis) Measure' came before Parliament in November 1926 for its sanction, the Measure was soundly defeated. The efforts of Blomfield were not, of course, solely responsible for this success, but his trenchant letters to *The Times* probably did much to awaken public opinion to the monstrous acts contemplated by the Church Assembly.

The championing of the City churches must have enhanced Blomfield's reputation, but unfortunately this took a severe blow at the beginning of the last decade of his life when he was commissioned to design an office building in Carlton Gardens.

The Carlton House Terrace Controversy

The building of Carlton House Terrace was a direct result of George IV's profligacy. He was presented with Carlton House itself, when, as Prince of Wales, he came of age in 1783. Over the next thirty years he spent enormous amounts of money enlarging and elaborating his palace in an attempt to put it on a par with the finest houses of Europe. However, it eventually proved inadequate and, one suspects, the Prince grew tired of it, with the result that upon his accession he determined to construct a new palace on the site of Buckingham House. In 1827 Carlton House was demolished, the columns of the portico being incorporated in the façade of the new National Gallery, and the gardens were given over to the construction of residential accommodation, comprising two blocks each of nine houses, with two extra houses added to the western end of the west block.

89 No. 4 Carlton Gardens

The architect for the new buildings was, needless to say, John Nash. Carlton House Terrace was one of his last major works and fittingly so, for the site was intrinsically important in the realisation of the great scheme of urban design involving the development of Regent's Park and Regent Street initiated by his royal patron. Indeed, the façade of Carlton House was meant to be the southern termination of the new street. With the house gone, it was decided to split the proposed terrace so that there was a way through to The Mall via a flight of steps, and to erect at the head of the flight Wyatt's Duke of York's Column, which would act as a focal point. Nash's chief concern was for overall effect on a large scale, and the details of the building (both from the aesthetic and constructional points of view) were very much second-

134

ary considerations, and what was created was a splendid piece of urban design of a type rarely seen in London.

The terrace proved to be successful and, over the years, its houses were occupied by various distinguished people, including a number of well-known statesmen. By the 1920s, however, the properties did not appear to be quite so desirable: some were vacant, some converted to new uses, others had conversions proposed. One of the houses, No. 4 Carlton Gardens, had been the home of A. J. Balfour and was unoccupied for two years following his death.

The Commissioners of Crown Lands, who administered Crown property, and were in effect landlords of the development, received a request in 1932 for a building lease on the site of No. 4. This was from a commercial concern, Pinchin, Johnson and Company Limited, wholesale paint manufacturers, who wished to build offices in the area. The Commissioners granted the request, pleased, one supposes, to have found an occupant for the site. Blomfield was appointed to design the new building. In order to optimise the value of what was an expensive lease, he proposed that the premises should be as high as the maximum the London Building Act allowed. The structure was thus to be eight stories high, probably half as high again as Nash's building, and constructed of a steel frame clad with Portland stone. The top two storeys were set back in order to lessen the apparent bulk and to provide a cornice height on the forward planes of the building not completely out of scale with those surrounding. In stylistic terms a stripped classicism, typical of commercial buildings of this period, was used, decorative devices being very sparingly applied and being limited to parapet urns, circular windows with swag motifs at sixth-floor level, and paired, double-height Ionic columns to the centre bays of the fourth and fifth floors. This scheme was submitted to the Royal Fine Art Commission for approval, which it received in July 1932. There were some queries about the proposed height, but it was made plain that the building would be useless to the owner unless carried up to the maximum allowed. The ease with which RFAC approval was gained was somewhat embarrassing, for Blomfield himself, of course, was a prominent member of the Commission. Queen Mary's blessing, required as she was occupant of the adjacent Marlborough House, was also given.

It now became clear that the Crown Commissioners were in favour of the overall removal of the fabric of Carlton House Terrace and its replacement with buildings more suited to modern commercial purposes. Blomfield's scheme for Carlton Gardens was a 'trial run'. He was asked to produce designs for the whole of a new Carlton House Terrace in accordance with the Carlton Gardens approach, and this he readily did. Work then proceeded directly with the removal of No. 4.

The demolition came as a surprise to many, and the occupant of a house opposite, Alfred Bossom, at one time an architect of skyscrapers in the United States and now a Member of Parliament, protested. Soon Sir John Squire

90 Proposal for the rebuilding of Carlton House Terrace. Drawing by Cyril Farey, 1932

and Sir Arthur Steel-Maitland were taking a leading rôle in a campaign to prevent desecration of Nash's work. Questions were asked in Parliament and many MPs signed a note of protest. It was rumoured that the Terrace would be turned into some kind of shopping street. In order to correct this impression and to enable the public to see what was proposed, Blomfield asked Cyril Farey to draw a perspective of the full design. This was then published in *The Times*. Instead of easing the situation it released a storm which was the worst that Blomfield had to weather during his long and turbulent career.

The Times became a focus for protest about the proposals, and was joined by the *Architects' Journal* and the *Architectural Review*, two of the most distinguished professional periodicals. Their rôle was not impartial, but aggressively pro-Nash and anti-Blomfield. When *The Times* published the perspective drawing, it was accompanied by an article heavily criticising the Crown Commissioners. From that time on, says Blomfield, of all the very many letters printed concerning the scheme, the only ones in support of the new proposals came from Blomfield himself.[8] In short, he stood alone in the columns of that august and well-respected newspaper, although his cause cannot have been helped by the fact that the principal proprietor of *The Times* lived in Carlton House Terrace.

The *Architects' Journal*, published weekly, contained anti-demolition pleas in each edition and its glossier sister, the monthly *Architectural Review*, decided to mount its own campaign. Not only did it print various articles condemning both the planned demolition and Blomfield's scheme, but it also wrote to a selection of people in the forefront of public life asking them to comment on the proposals and to answer three questions of its own formulation.[9] The questions were phrased in order to elicit the response so clearly hoped for by the *Architectural Review*. In the January edition it printed almost fifty replies, from people as diverse as Max Beerbohm, Aldous Huxley,

Charles B. Cochran, Hilaire Belloc, and Kenneth Clark, all deploring what was to happen. Not content with this, the *Review*, with which Blomfield had been closely associated in its earliest days, proceeded to attack him personally. Quotations from Blomfield's own writings were used to an ironic end and were prominently included next to photographs of the Terrace. In the February edition of 1933, Osbert Burdett talked of 'the massacre of the whole terrace, planned by Sir Reginald Blomfield with the ardour of a sportsman exulting in the thought of bringing down the most beautiful thing within his range'. There is, further, talk of 'Sir Reginald and his kind' wishing to destroy old buildings.[10]

The unmitigated relish with which Blomfield was attacked was hardly surprising. After years of pontification on all matters architectural, here was a chance to get back at a man who had attempted to establish himself as an *arbiter elegantiarum*, someone who had not hesitated to use his undoubted literary gifts against anyone he thought worth fighting. The *Architectural Review*, for instance, was one of the foremost proponents of the Modern Movement, against which Blomfield often used the full force of his argument. Even so, the early months of 1933 must have been a testing time for him, standing alone and condemned by his most distinguished contemporaries. This kind of attack may have served to strengthen the resolve of a committed revolutionary, but Blomfield was a pillar of the establishment. The campaign reached its height with a meeting in Caxton Hall on 5 February 1933, when it was made known that the protestors now had the backing of both the President of the Royal Academy and the Archbishop of Canterbury. Their main objections fell into two categories: opposition to the design of No. 4, Carlton Gardens, particularly with reference to its height and finish material and opposition to the destruction of fine and significant architecture and its replacement with something inferior. It must have become very clear to the Government that their plans could not go ahead smoothly. Consequently, they appointed a committee under Lord Gorell, which would advise and control the administration of all Crown lands in London. As a result of the Committee's deliberations, it was decided that nothing was to be done with Carlton House Terrace for twenty-five years. There the matter ended, the protestors had been victorious, though they did not succeed in halting the construction of No. 4, Carlton Gardens before completion, as many wished to do. It stands today, as a rather grey, austere reminder of what might have been.

The unfortunate controversy did nothing to enhance Blomfield's reputation, though it is true to say that he was already a 'villain' as far as the young generation of architects was concerned. It did not lessen his resolve to go into battle in other causes. He felt no shame in suggesting the destruction of Nash's work, for he not only thought Nash's architecture despicable, but also completely unsuitable for adaptation to modern purposes. The largeness of concept of the urban design which he admired would, he felt, be retained by his own new proposals. He did not retreat, and one has to admire the resolve of a man, by now seventy-six years old, who would not be crushed or driven into a bitter retirement by such an onslaught.

The Carlton House Terrace affair was a sad interlude in Blomfield's career, but it must be seen against the background of his increasing interest in urban design, or 'town planning' as he called it, particularly in London. This interest had led to an involvement with the Thames bridges, essential parts of the capital's traffic flow schemes, and important elements in its townscape.

London's Bridges

Blomfield's first major association with bridge design had come during the First World War. In 1916, he was involved with Sir Aston Webb and John Burns in putting forward a new scheme for the redevelopment of Charing Cross Bridge. This had been mooted for many years, but the intention of the railway company to repair and strengthen the existing bridge prompted Blomfield and his colleagues to take action. The scheme which they proposed was grandiose and was rejected as being too expensive. Nevertheless, it was the precursor of many subsequent projects and heralded seventeen years of wrangling, committees and reports. Blomfield was deeply involved in much of this business, but what is important is not the history and politics of the affair, but the fact that he made constant pleas for an overall urban design policy and the necessity for a sensitive and comprehensive approach.

This initial scheme suggested a grand roadway to run in an uninterrupted straight line from St Martin's-in-the-Fields to the junction of Waterloo Road with York Road, and a transplanting of the railway station and hotel to the south side of the Thames. This would be enhanced by a large open 'place' facing onto the river. Although this proposal was dropped, Blomfield retained an interest in the scheme and there was a flurry of letter writing to *The Times* in 1925–26 when he suggested that there should be a new bridge at Charing Cross, but that the station and hotel should remain in their existing positions. Little notice was taken of this suggestion, but the LCC did set up a Commission in 1928 to look into the problem. No action was taken upon the advice of the Commission, and so the matter lay dormant as far as Blomfield was concerned, until late 1929 when in a surprise move the LCC put forward a scheme which it hoped to implement the following year. This scheme was not generally liked and Blomfield helped to organise opposition to it. It was eventually rejected by Parliament.

The next move was in 1930 when the LCC set up an Advisory Committee, upon which Blomfield represented the Royal Academy. He took this opportunity to propose a scheme of his own. The existing railway bridge was to be retained and a new suspension bridge built, 'with a roadway leading in

91 A drawing of one of the towers for the proposed Charing Cross suspension bridge, 1930

a continuous straight line from a 'Place' in the Strand opposite Charing Cross Hospital to another great 'Place' at the intersection of Waterloo Road with York Road and Stamford Street'.[11]

The new bridge was to have a span of 800 feet, and a width of 80 feet. It was approached on either side through two huge 'triumphal arch' towers to which the suspension cables were attached. Blomfield had worked out the design in some detail, and published perspective drawings in September 1930: one, a general view of the bridge indicating its relationship to the river and surroundings, the other showing, in detail, one of the towers. These were to be of stone, austere and massive but diminishing in bulk towards the top. The road entered the bridge via a coffered arch and there were footways to either side of the arch, which was supported by Doric columns. In style it was somewhat similar to the Menin Gate. The design was rejected, and in any event the towers were much too heavy and pompous, and negated any of the inherent elegance and lightness to be expected from a suspension bridge.

There the matter closed for Blomfield, and the advice of the committee upon which he sat was neglected.[12] The old railway bridge is still there today, but the LCC eventually found other ways of dealing with the problems of cross-river traffic.

The problem was resolved by demolishing old Waterloo Bridge, and replacing it by a new bridge, six lanes wide. Indeed, the proposals for Charing Cross Station and its bridge were intertwined with the destiny of old Waterloo Bridge, which was greatly admired by many. In the early 1920s it had suffered some subsidence, which was not helped by the rather clumsy attempts of LCC engineers to rectify the problem, and an ugly temporary bridge was built alongside. By 1926, however, the LCC had decided that it should be demolished. Blomfield was at first opposed to such moves, but eventually was prepared to accept the end of the bridge, and to act as an assessor, together with Sir Giles Gilbert Scott, in an open competition for the design of a new one.[13] However, there was an appeal to his artistic conscience, and he once again joined the anti-demolition lobby, though Scott remained, and was eventually given the commission for the new bridge. He involved himself in the writing of letters and other protests, and produced a scheme for the widening of the old bridge. It was first presented to the 'Cross River Traffic Commission' in 1926, but reappeared when it looked as though the LCC might, instead of demolition, widen the existing bridge to four lanes in 1932. Blomfield's drawing was illustrated in *The Times*, exhibited at the Royal Academy and a model of the proposal was displayed on the staging of the temporary bridge. His idea was to corbel out by three and a half feet from either side of the bridge, which, he said, would hardly be noticeable from any further than a little distance and would retain the existing lines and details of the bridge.

The LCC's move to put its demolition plan into operation suffered what appeared to be an irrevocable setback when Parliament decided not to grant sixty per cent of the necessary cost for the finance of the new bridge. In the *Memoirs*, published in 1932, Blomfield looks forward to the widening of the old bridge and considers it as saved. The LCC, however, persevered. Its members were due to vote on the future of the bridge in mid-February 1932. The letter columns of *The Times* became busy, Blomfield writing no less than five times between January and April of that year. Other letters included an extremely scathing one from D. S. MacColl, and a plea to councillors to vote against demolition by the Secretary of the 'London Society'. The architectural consultant to the Council, Sir Edwin Lutyens, though, appeared to have little concern for the bridge and, in any case, had been commissioned by the Ministry of Transport to design a new combined road and rail bridge for Charing Cross.

Unfortunately, the LCC voted in favour of demolition, and although opposed by the Government, whose Royal Commission had decided in favour of retaining the bridge, the LCC eventually succeeded in bringing about its

WATERLOO BRIDGE·
as widened 7.6
by corbels 3.6 on each side
to take four lines
of traffic

92 The project for widening Waterloo Bridge by corbelling, 1932

removal, costs for all works being met from the rates. Herbert Morrison, leader of the Council, gleefully removed the first stones of Rennie's masterpiece himself. Work now began on its replacement with the new structure, which was of reinforced concrete, clad in stone and designed by the engineer Sir Frederick Palmer together with Sir Giles Gilbert Scott. It had already been condemned by the Royal Fine Art Commission, and Blomfield himself felt that its lines did not accord with those of its surroundings. He had little choice, however, but to accept the replacement of 'architecturally the finest bridge in England, if not the world'.[14] In his biography of Norman Shaw he includes the following quotation:

> As early as 1896 [Shaw] wrote, 'Waterloo Bridge, as it stands, is second in importance only to St Paul's and must be preserved at any cost and sacrifice'. If the LCC had only heeded these words, we should have been spared the odious crime of its destruction, the most damnable Municipal blunder in the whole history of London.[15]

The history of London's cross-river traffic in those inter-war years is complex and, it seems, not without the suggestion of opportunism and self-interest on behalf of some of the architects involved.

Blomfield's interest in London's bridges only really bore fruit in one case, Lambeth Bridge. It was built to replace the existing and extremely ugly suspension bridge of 1862, which had been erected very cheaply and was certainly not appropriate for its important position. It was open only to pedestrian traffic for many years prior to its demolition in 1929, thereby exacerbating the increasing traffic-flow problems of the metropolis.

Blomfield's first design for the bridge was displayed at the Royal Academy

93 Study for the south approach, Lambeth Bridge, 1925. At this stage the bridge was entirely stone faced

94 Lambeth Bridge, as completed

in 1925. He was working in conjunction with G. Topham Forrest, architect to the LCC, and Sir George Humphreys, the engineer. Blomfield recalled: 'very wisely I was called in at an early date to say how the elevations were to be treated.'[16]

Sir George Humphreys was responsible for the constructional design of the bridge. This was to be in steel, and both the 1925 version and the final version had five arches spanning, in all, over 700 feet.[17] The first design used granite cladding, with granite-faced reinforced concrete under the footways and steel girders supporting the roadway. Later on, however, Blomfield was convinced by Humphreys that his kind of composite construction was not very satisfactory, and so the reinforced concrete and granite were eliminated from the superstructure. The piers remained granite, but Blomfield now had the problem of disguising the steel skeleton as it ran between the piers. He hit on the idea of using steel plating, analogous to ship construction. The result is remarkable, especially in its contrast between the smooth, curved, massive piers, and the flat, plated panels over the arches.

Apart from the elevations, he also designed the approaches, parapets and obelisks at the entrance to the bridge. The designs for these were much simplified before the final version was built, fortunately in the case of the obelisks, which changed in character from bulbous statuary-topped ornateness to a clean geometric austerity.

The bridge was started in 1929, completed in 1932, and opened by King George V on 19 July of that year, amidst much publicity. A good deal of attention was paid by the popular press to the new structure and its designer but it is ironic to note that the *Daily Sketch* contrasted Blomfield's work with the old Waterloo Bridge, which he was desperately trying to save:

> Having taken a look at the new Lambeth Bridge . . . and at Waterloo
> Bridge . . . what is your verdict on the beauty aspect of the Waterloo
> Bridge controversy?
> There are those that say that the Old Lady of Waterloo has a mellow
> charm. . . . Others challenge that view by pointing to the smart young
> lady of Lambeth.[18]

It may be that the success of Lambeth Bridge hastened the decline of Waterloo Bridge.

Following in the wake of the Lambeth Bridge commission, Blomfield was involved in the design of two more bridge projects in the late 1920s. These were at Stratford-upon-Avon and Rotherham.

The Rotherham bridge dates from 1927 and was carried out with Blomfield as architectural consultant to Vincent Turner, the Borough Engineer. The new bridge was built of reinforced concrete with a single span of 94 feet, to carry vehicular traffic. The Gothic 'Chantry Bridge' with its adjoining chapel

95 The reconstruction of Chantry Bridge, Rotherham in conjunction with Vincent Turner, by Gordon Holt, 1927

no longer spanned the river, but was stopped-off with a right-angled return to the new bridge, taking pedestrians only. Blomfield was instrumental in this work, and in the design and construction of stone parapets to the new bridge. Much effort was put into restoration of the old bridge and in the re-use of the old stone elements.

Blomfield's unexecuted design for Stratford appeared in the following year and was very different in character.[19] It had five main elliptical spans, and was in brick with stone dressings. The entrance to the bridge was guarded by two whimsical little towers of brick and stone, with cupola roofs and wind vanes, reminiscent of those he had used some years earlier in his scheme for the Eyot Bridge at Shepperton. This structure was to have a reinforced-concrete arch of 90-foot span, with the pavilions at either end. These features are attractive, but hardly in keeping with the very straight-forward and unembellished concrete bridge.

Blomfield's willingness to use modern techniques was not inconsistent with his philosophical outlook. He would clearly use any appropriate means to achieve his aesthetic aims. In the case of bridges, though, where engineering

96 Project for a new bridge, Stratford upon Avon, 1928. The proposed
Shakespeare Memorial Theatre is shown in the background

technology becomes a dominant generator of form, his efforts at times tend
towards the cosmetic. In the broad context of urban design, however, the
design of bridges can be seen as the architect's responsibility, and Blomfield
had already made a plea for this in *The Touchstone of Architecture*. A bridge
is, after all, one of the most potent symbols in the fabric of the city and its
visual qualities are important in helping to provide a particular sense of place.

The basis of visual acceptability, though, was undergoing a profound
change at this time. Blomfield did not submit gracefully to the overwhelming
pressure that was exerted, but decided to fight the Modern Movement with
all his might.

97 Project for a reinforced concrete bridge, The Eyot, Shepperton, 1921

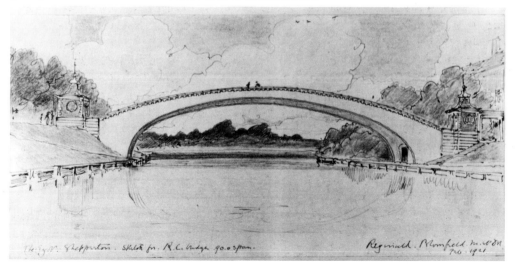

CHAPTER 8
CONFLICTS AND
CONCLUSIONS

Blomfield is best remembered today for his attacks on 'modern' architecture and the 'International Style'. This may be because the profession has been dominated by a generation of architects to whom, at one time, he was a bogey-man; someone who represented reaction and conservatism in the face of youthful enthusiasm for the 'New Architecture'. His polemic against modern art, *Modernismus*, published in 1934, is one of his best-known books, yet it is only a small part of his literary output and it should not be seen out of context.[1] Blomfield had commented upon contemporary design from his earliest days, in books, lectures and papers, and it is clear that old age did not prevent him from continuing his practice.

The New Architecture

Although cast in the rôle of a reactionary, Blomfield was by no means opposed to technological progress, as the construction and servicing of his buildings bear out. In spite of any corners into which he may have been thrust during the 'traditionalist versus modernist' debate, he did not object to machines, and would always use a convenient modern method whenever available. In an address given at the opening of the 1913–14 RIBA session he expounded:

> The arts do not stand still – architecture the least of all . . . it is essentially a practical art. Fresh problems present themselves in planning, provision has to be made for the ever widening range of applied mechanical science, new methods of construction have to be considered, the practice of architecture becomes more difficult every year, and the modern architect has to deal with a range of subjects that would have paralysed his grandfather.

The other side of the coin, however, is shown in the same address: 'It is time to give up conscious attempts at originality . . . where our critics go wrong is in demanding a new language when they ought to be demanding new ideas. The old language will do very well if we are masters of it.'[2] His attitude was that the old classical language should be used, modified, perhaps, to take in new developments, needs and uses. There should be no seeking after sensational modes of expression. He was in favour of evolution rather than revolution.

Blomfield, though, had pioneered the move away from the ornate and eclectic architecture of the late nineteenth century. In the words of Sir Charles Reilly, 'Blomfield swept the board of this ill-digested stuff'. He was interested in a return to what he saw as the fundamentals of architecture: balance, mass, outline, consistency and 'a power of imagination that rises superior to the entanglements of detail'. In this dismissal of ill-conceived and futile detail Blomfield had much in common with the modernists, or 'Modernismists' as he preferred to call them:

> Our 'new architects' will probably not admit it in view of my criticisms
> of their efforts, but in point of fact, by opening fire on the revivalists
> and the silly sentimentality of the last century, I provided them with
> an open way along which architecture might advance. Unfortunately,
> they have ignored the teaching of history and taken the wrong turning.[3]

What were Blomfield's objections, then, to the 'new architecture'? They were based on his beliefs that the new movement encouraged cosmopolitanism, and he believed that any nation's architecture must reflect its heritage and temperament; that it was founded on a suspect dogma which worshipped functionalism and the machine; and that it rejected the past totally and looked for a new aesthetic not based on any recognisable architectural precedent. It was on these grounds that he attacked the movement. This he did trenchantly and wittily, citing many examples, and ridiculing any which were open to such treatment. Some of his pronouncements were exaggerated and foolish, some humourous, and others full of common sense and entirely to the point. Many of these, designed to irritate the 'Modernismists', have with the passage of time proved to be only too true.

The attacks were undertaken through addresses and lectures, written articles, dialogues, debates and, of course, books.[4] He had made statements in *The Touchstone of Architecture* and, in passing, in the *Memoirs*, but the chief work was *Modernismus*.[5] This 'little book' was a compendium of some of Blomfield's more outrageous pronouncements about modern art. It was written because he felt bound to do what he could 'to rescue a noble art from the degradation into which it seems to be sinking.'[6]

It discussed not only modern architecture, but also the Baroque, and modern sculpture, painting, music and letters. It concluded with an indication of 'the way home'.

Unfortunately, as with nearly all of Blomfield's attacks upon 'Modernismus', it was indiscriminate and aimed at diverse targets. In the same breath it mentioned the pronouncements of 'Herr Cohen-Portheim', 'M. Le Corbusier' and 'Herr Mendelsohn'. The attacks on painting and sculpture were similarly unselective. It is easy to criticise Blomfield for this from our present standpoint, although, even at the time, it must have been apparent that there were several different philosophies, and not all of their exponents were charlatans, Bolsheviks or attention seekers. He often took remarks out of context to furnish a series of easy targets. As the architect Amyas Connell remarked: 'You have admirably demonstrated, Sir Reginald, the old truth that in a few minutes fallacies can be uttered which may take a lifetime to demolish.'[7]

Perhaps the least acceptable of Blomfield's remarks concerned the political threat of the new movement and the danger of its Continental origin. 'I do not myself believe that such a great and permanent art as Architecture can be finally lost in the quicksands of Bolshevism', he wrote; '[the new architects draw] inspiration from the creations of contemporary French, German, Austrian and American architects. Whatever merits they may have are alien to the English tradition and temperament.'[8]

Although this is an extreme and reactionary view, it must be remembered that when Blomfield talked of the 'tyranny of communism' and also 'whether this movement is Hitlerism or Bolshevism, Fascism or Communism, is immaterial',[9] unfashionable as this would seem to contemporary intellectuals, he was very near the truth. Terror reigned both in Stalin's Russia and Hitler's Germany and apostles of the International Style were not really welcome in either country.

These are the ostensible grounds on which Blomfield based his dislike of the 'new architecture'. It may be that, in part, they are a rationalisation of a deeper fear. The strength and breadth of Blomfield's attack leads one to concur with Amyas Connell: 'You are afraid of the present phase of evolution because you can neither understand nor use it. . . . I suggest that you look upon modern architecture with a vision distorted by fear'. One cannot agree, however, with Connell's explanation of this: 'What you really seem to dislike and fear is efficiency'.[10] Such a statement is relative to Connell's defence of the dogma of the Modern Movement. Blomfield was certainly not an inefficient man, as the success of both his practice and public life proves. It may be suggested, though, that the fear was based on his long held theory of the artist-architect. To Blomfield, beauty was governed by criteria established over the centuries and stretching back to the foundations of civilisation. The 'Modernismists', were claiming that beauty and inspiration were to be found in all sorts of things that were not previously considered as having any aesthetic merit. If the whole foundation of beauty and the arts was to be changed, how could the artist-architect, who had founded his work on good taste and the old orders, survive, and was not the whole structure of Blomfield's philosophy shaken? As he put it in a lecture at the Royal Academy:

As thoughtful persons we undoubtedly derive satisfaction from
machinery that fulfils the purpose for which it has been constructed,
but this is an entirely different feeling from the thrill that we feel
instantaneously and spontaneously from beauty in any shape, beauty of

the human form, of the sea and the land, of cloud and sunshine, of noble buildings and great works of art.[11]

This was, perhaps, the main stumbling block in Blomfield's acceptance of modern design. Yet in his criticisms of 'Modernismus' he struck many a true note and now that disillusion with the Modern Movement has become apparent they seem especially pointed and relevant. Examples are plentiful:

> The result of the continuous line of windows (a favourite trick of the new manner much affected by Herr Mendelsohn) must be that the partition walls of the rooms run out into the windows, without any returns, with no place where you can keep out of the draught, or if necessary, out of the light. What happens when summer heat is 80° and in winter it is 20° below freezing point?[12]

Blomfield mentions modern materials: The fact is that concrete, whether reinforced or not, is a material of rather doubtful value for public or domestic buildings.[13]

There are various other examples of such good sense, overlooked by 'Modernismists' in their desire to express their new philosophies.

During the last years of his life the general enthusiasm among architects and critics for the 'new architecture' increased. Blomfield looked with bitterness upon the schools of architecture in particular, especially as he had been closely involved with many of them in their formative years. Sir Charles Reilly, Head of Liverpool School of Architecture, remarked in his memoirs: 'Now I fear he thinks the Schools are all Bolshevik institutions badly bitten with 'Modernismus', as he calls modern design, and that I too am tainted. I hope I am, for I like still to be alive.'[14]

Blomfield did not capitulate, however. At one stage insult was added to injury with the construction of a 'Modernismist' house virtually on his doorstep. This was No. 66, Frognal, Hampstead, just over the road from Blomfield's own house, No. 51. The new house was designed by Connell, Ward and Lucas. Amyas Connell had been Blomfield's opponent in the somewhat acrimonious debate quoted earlier and Blomfield had also found fault with him when he designed his famous 'High and Over' house for Professor Bernard Ashmole in Buckinghamshire, asking what was the use of the Rome Scholarship if Connell were to end up 'flouting the face of authority'.

Blomfield was not, therefore, well disposed either to the architects or the design of the house, and he did not let its building go ahead without a fight, in which other residents, such as the architect Adrian Gilbert Scott, took part on Blomfield's side. They protested strongly, and many conditions were eventually made by the local authority in terms of the colour and decoration of the building. Connell, Ward and Lucas had a stubborn client, however, who was determined that the house should be built as designed, and so it was. The legal wrangles were skilfully dealt with, and Blomfield lost one of his last fights.

He did not give up hope for the future of English architecture, though, and in his last major publication *Richard Norman Shaw, RA* (1940) he stated optimistically: 'I nurse the unconquerable hope that out of this chaotic welter of experiment and failure our English tradition will again emerge chastised and fortified by adversity.'[15]

Blomfield was consoled by the view that perhaps 'Modernismus' was only a passing fashion, like Lethaby who talked of 'ye olde modern style'. In 'The New Architecture' he cited instances of the sacrifices of dogma for the sake of appearance. For example: 'The design of the Potsdam Observatory was supposed to be dictated by reinforced concrete, but unfortunately the supply of steel rods failed, and I am told the buildings had to be constructed mainly in brick.'[16]

He placed his trust in the future: 'I think the new architecture will go the way of other fashions. What is good in it will be absorbed, and the rest of it relegated to the dustbin.'[17]

It now seems that this trust was not wholly misplaced.

Vespertine Ventures

Blomfield continued to do battle with 'Modernismus' and to snipe at other worthy targets throughout the remaining years of his life, but ironically he became involved with the design of one of the icons of modernism, the electricity transmission tower, or 'pylon'. The Central Electricity Board had been set up in the mid 1920s to co-ordinate the generation and distribution of electric power. Mindful of the concern, expressed in some quarters, about the effects on the already embattled countryside of the network of towers and cables, the Board appointed Blomfield to advise on the design of the pylons. An example from the United States was chosen in the first instance, and it was modified so that its proportions became acceptable, and the whole thing looked more stable. Blomfield's plea for the addition of extra curves, though, was rejected on grounds of cost, Nevertheless, the form that resulted became a familiar sight, and was even celebrated by the modernist poet Stephen Spender. Blomfield's contribution must have been valued by the Board, for later, in 1929, he was appointed as landscape consultant to advise on the siting of power lines, especially in sensitive areas of natural beauty.[18]

The close liaison with the Central Electricity Board again emphasises the fact that Blomfield's quarrel was not with modern technology, but with the design philosophy of the Modern Movement. He did not confine his misgivings about modernism to architecture. He attacked exhibitions of modern industrial art and painting, and was puzzled by Joyce's literature and Britten's music.[19] Of the International Surrealist Exhibition, staged in 1936, he commented that 'the result would be amusing, if it was not so profoundly mischievous'.[20] He does not seem to have lost any opportunity to write to *The Times* or *The Daily Telegraph* on subjects concerned with new attitudes to the arts, especially if to do with buildings.[21]

In the mid 1930s he was active in his home district of Hampstead, trying to form a bulwark against the incursions of speculative builders. He became chairman of a society of architects resident in the borough who were to advise the Council on such subjects as the preservation of old houses. In fact, one of the most distinguished members of the society, Stanley Adshead, was to lose his late-Georgian house to make way for a block of flats. Clearly, the architects were concerned about changes of character in the area and must have been even more appalled at the prospect of the proposed Connell, Ward and Lucas project in Frognal. Adrian Gilbert Scott noted that 'what might look suitable on the Great West-road can look quite incongruous and out of place in a quiet Georgian residential district'.[22]

Blomfield's involvement in local politics became more pronounced in December 1936, when at the age of 80 he was elected President of the Hampstead Municipal Electors' Association. It is interesting to note that Sir Philip Chetwode's Local Ratepayers' Association, a rival body, was considered to be much more right-wing than Blomfield's group, and that with local elections pending it was feared that candidates put forward by both associations would split the Conservative vote and allow the Socialists to gain control.

Blomfield's activities, therefore, did not diminish in scope during the last years of his life, even if his work in practice slowed down. He was in partnership with his son, Austin, and the number of designs he produced became fewer. Also, long-running projects, such as Lady Margaret Hall, were terminated. The Headrow, though, was being constructed throughout most of this period and there was a further extension to the United University Club. His last individual design was probably for the gates of St James's Church, Piccadilly. The original entrance had been removed in order to make way for spectator stands at the Coronation of King George VI. With money raised from the hire of these stands to the public, funds were provided for new gates, and these were installed in the autumn of 1937. The design included wrought-iron work for the gates themselves, as well as the brick and stone piers, all, of course, in the 'Wrenaissance' style. This project forms a neat conclusion to Blomfield's career. His earliest research had concerned the history of wrought iron and some of his successful early designs were executed in the material. He must have been pleased with the result, but unfortunately the church and its surroundings were badly damaged by bombing early in the Second World War, and the gates were taken away.

Reminiscence and Recollection

A large proportion of Blomfield's written work in these last years tends to concern itself with reminiscence. Most notable from this point of view is, of course, *Memoirs of an Architect*, published in 1932, but his biography of Norman Shaw is also heavily laced with personal recollections and reflections. The *Memoirs*, which appeared ten years before his death, chronicle his life, but the treatment of subjects is unevenly weighted. In some cases, important developmental stages are omitted, whilst whole sections are devoted to sporting contests of one kind or another. This may well infuriate the Blomfield scholar, but it is indicative of the kind of man that Blomfield was. Minor personalities and sporting friends, particularly if titled, are treated to whole paragraphs, whilst the reader longs in vain for comment on professional contemporaries and outstanding figures in the world of the arts. Nevertheless, the whole amalgam is very readable and entertaining, and there are several instances of sarcastic wit. There is also an astonishing lack of modesty and Blomfield does not hesitate to include many of the more favourable comments received about both his work and himself. His direct, and to some extent naïve nature comes through clearly in the book. Certainly, all the events recorded are seen from one angle, and there is little perspective, or representation of occurrences in the round. Towards the end of the volume there is too much about committee work to give an entertaining balance.

The short biography of Norman Shaw was Blomfield's final book. If it is lacking in content, or ill-balanced, or even, as some have maintained, unworthy of its subject, it must be remembered that Blomfield was eighty-three at the time of its publication in 1940. It must also be remembered that at that time Norman Shaw was almost forgotten, or at least despised by the new generation; yet Blomfield maintained that Shaw was a great and important architect. In the preface he states:

> To Shaw, more than anyone is due the recovery of architecture from the dull conventions of the Victorian era, and the advance of the best architecture of our time on the lines of the English tradition of the 18th century . . . but no memoir of Shaw's life and work has yet been written, and as one of the few men living who knew him personally, I pay this tribute to his memory before it is too late.

Blomfield adds that in his view 'only one architect had any claim to carry the mantle of Wren and that was Richard Norman Shaw'.[23]

The information about Shaw is far from exhaustive, and in the rather slim volume Blomfield takes a large amount of space to recount his own attitudes to subjects ranging from Ruskin to 'Modernismus'. He also writes about Shaw's pupils, assistants and friends, and the book is a useful source of information for those interested in the 'family'. If it is a disappointment, we must forgive an old man who devoted his last full-length literary work to one of Britain's foremost nineteenth-century architects with the object of according him his rightful position. Shaw is now, happily, reinstated.

An All-Round Man

Richard Norman Shaw, RA was Sir Reginald Blomfield's last major work. The closing years of his life brought some sadness and bitterness as well as continued friendships. There was little diminution of the fighting spirit and a remarkable ability to continue with creative work and sporting interests to within a few months of the end. Blomfield was valued by many as a robust and ebullient character, undaunted by his years, who refused to succumb to old age. No doubt, he was a symbol of the hope that they, too, would continue to be active well past the prescribed three score years and ten. As early as July 1929, at the age of 72, Blomfield was subject of an article in *The Daily Chronicle*, 'What keeps us young', where he extolled the virtues of slow but sure development, moderation in food and drink and, of course the philosophy of '*mens sana in corpore sano*'. Other attributes were also required, though:

> But the real way to keep young is to preserve as wide a range of interests as possible, interest not only in sports and amusement, but in literature, art and music, science, too, though I am quite unscientific. . . .
> The Humanist alone, taking the term in its widest sense, seems to me to have the key. The vital force that keeps man going is not solely physical and material, it is spiritual as well, a certain ethical and intellectual attitude to life and all that it means.

This 'all-round man' was honoured by his club with a celebratory dinner when he reached the age of eighty. The menu at the Athenaeum on the night of Monday, 21 December 1936, included *Consommé Laureat*, *Filet de Sole à l'Académie*, *Bombe glacée aux beaux arts*, and *Diable à Cheval*, which one supposes, was a punning reference to Blomfield's hunting experiences. The toasts were proposed by Lord Macmillan, Blomfield's publisher, and W. Curtis Green, a friend and fellow architect, demonstrating that although his aggressive and forthright manner could cause him to make enemies, Blomfield was well respected in certain influential circles. It may be that in an age when manners were more greatly valued than truth, he could easily become unpopular. This, indeed, was probably the case at the Royal Academy, where his last years seem to have been rather unhappy. When an opportunity presented itself for yet another attempt to gain the Presidency he found that he was debarred by the age limit.[24] His chagrin was further increased when Lutyens

was elected. Meetings must have been frustrating, for Lutyens was no committee man, and it would have been uncharacteristic if Blomfield had not made
his frustration felt. Indeed, even in 1942, the last year of Blomfield's life,
Lutyens records, in a letter to his wife, that Blomfield had attacked him at
an Academy meeting.[25]

However, personal conflicts were soon put into perspective by those of a
national scale with the outbreak of the Second World War. It is unfortunate
that the last three years of Blomfield's life should have occurred during this
period of privation. His health did not really begin to fail until 1941, and
during the early years of the war he found enough energy to visit his office,
where the practice was being continued by Austin Blomfield, for an hour or
so at least once each week. He sustained self-inflicted wounds twice: first when
he broke his arm by falling from a wall whilst cutting a hedge, and then when
he shook himself severely by jumping onto the rear platform of a bus that
was moving off, and landing heavily in the road. However, he recovered from
these physical shocks and, during his last summer, he visited Lords, where
his enthusiasm for cricket was seen to be undiminished. He received a
devastating blow at about this time, though, with the death of his daughter,
Isabella. She had long suffered from ill-health, but although he also had two
sons, one of whom was to carry on his practice until 1969, the other of whom
was a clergyman, the pain of losing an offspring must have been severe.

Blomfield could not really help the war effort, as he had in the First World
War, by joining a band of volunteers and enthusiastically supervising trench
construction, yet he tried as best he could. Unfortunately, there was a call
for scrap paper and he diligently went through his drawings, carefully noting
the name of each scheme in a book and bundling the papers ready for disposal.
Only two or three bundles seem to have escaped. During this time his property
suffered, the office at New Court was set on fire by an incendiary bomb, but
was not totally gutted; his house in Frognal sustained some slight bomb
damage, and army occupation was unkind to Point Hill and some of his smaller
properties in Rye. Yet even in the gloom of a wartime autumn and within
months of his death, his creative spark still glimmered. He wrote a poem,
published in *The Times* in November 1942, which apparently evoked a
sympathetic response from many elderly people. It was 'The Cry of the Aged':

'Tis not for us to join the furious fray,
Or face the dangers of the sea, or dive
From Heaven's enormous height, and ruthless pour
Death and destruction on the accursed foe,
These things are not for us: but we can do
The day's work in the day, and carry on
Cheerful and uncomplaining, and endure
Hunger and cold, if such must be our lot;

And to our utmost help to bear the cost
Of the vast burdens of the wearied State –
We cannot fight, but still old age may say,
'They also serve, who only stand and wait.'

Among the many letters received congratulating him on this publication were those from the distinguished painters W. Russell Flint and his old friend George Clausen. It was a gratifying response to this, his last piece of recorded work.[26]

Reginald Blomfield died at his house in Frognal shortly after his eighty-sixth birthday on 27 December 1942. There is no doubt that in the last year of his life he knew that death was approaching and that his physical infirmities were growing worse, but it is also certain that his mind was still active and that his interest in life and creativity was still strong. This time, though, he had no option but to lose the fight and to submit gracefully to the inevitable.

CHAPTER 9
EVALUATION

It would be too strong a statement to say that Blomfield's death at the end of 1942 came as a shock. He was an old man and, besides, the appalling consequences of war had blunted the nation's emotional responses. The obituary notices, however, signify a sense of loss, as though a seemingly permanent institution had suddenly been removed. This was compounded by the fact that even up to the end of his life he had remained energetic and active. For decades his voice had pronounced unfailingly on all aspects of architecture and design, and legions of students had been exposed to his architectural theories. Many of the older generation thought of him as a guardian of values, whilst to the youngsters he was an increasing irritant. All in all he was a rock-like figure, and one of the few architects capable of representing his profession ably within the sphere of national affairs.

Blomfield's powerful personality was, in fact, one of the chief factors in his success. Some architects, though talented, are introverted and narrow in outlook; some are intuitive rather than academic in approach. Blomfield, by harnessing his intellectual and personal qualities, could dominate situations and succeed where other equally creative men may have failed. He was able to fulfil to the highest degree all the varied rôles demanded of the architect, becoming, in the words of his erstwhile pupil, A. Trystan Edwards, 'the complete architect'.[1]

Blomfield was an excellent draughtsman and a very competent constructor of buildings. He could cope well with business affairs and took a leading rôle in professional politics. He was both practical and imaginative and, above all, he had a command of language and argument that is denied to most architects, and is to be envied even by those who make their living through the written word. The full exploitation of all these charcteristics was made possible by what Sir Albert Richardson called his 'productive energy'.[2] Unhampered, one supposes, by any personal doubts, Blomfield produced an enormous quantity of work throughout his life. He sought challenges and enjoyed fights, and his relaxation involved hard competitive sports. There is no question of the intensity of his response to the arts, and he always described himself as an artist, but he was the antithesis of the languid sensualist or the self-indulgent bohemian. He cared deeply about the 'mistress art' and devoted much time to her well-being and protection, time that could have been spent in more obvious forms of professional advancement.

Those meeting Blomfield would have found a 'tall, commanding figure, physically striking, intellectually impressive'[3], but they may have been taken aback by a certain aggression and abruptness in his manner. He had always been prone to attacks of bad temper and he did not suffer fools gladly, an attitude which occasionally led him to lose clients.[4] There are various anecdotes about this lack of control. Once, when presented with a cold and tasteless dinner, he hurled the meal back at the cook, plate and all. His telephone manner was forbidding in the extreme, as though he resented the intrusiveness and insistence of the bell.[5] It is well known, also, that he kept a hassock in his billiards room to kick when he missed a shot, and he rarely moderated his language in times of stress.[6] He bore few grudges once the outburst was past, however, though he did lose friends. Indeed, it is fairly evident that he was shocked and puzzled by persons of a more calculating nature. He was direct and almost naïve in his approach to life, and this had the advantage of leaving his mind free to concentrate upon business and professional matters. He has been described as 'an aggressive and unpleasant man', yet this is surely a distorted opinion.[7] Blomfield's temper and impatience went hand in hand with his dynamism and productive energy.

This extraordinary personality, then, marked Blomfield out from most of his contemporaries, but it is interesting to compare him with them as an architect pure and simple. First, it must be said that he did not produce a consistent standard of design. Some of his buildings are unrefined, others lack inspiration. Less well-known architects were often more reliable in producing a high level of work, but they probably confined their efforts to one or two building types, specialising in domestic design and never tackling large-scale structures. Furthermore, they may never have developed stylistically, as Blomfield did, with the inevitable result that their work was fashionable for a decade or so and then disappeared as circumstances changed.

It is certain, though, that inspiration did not command Blomfield's pencil to the extent that it did those of natural and instinctive designers. The greatest of these was Sir Edwin Lutyens (1869–1944). Lutyens, although working at the same time as Blomfield, was more than twelve years younger. He had not had the formal education so prized by the older man, and came to prominence as a designer of houses scarcely later than Blomfield. The two architects differed greatly in outlook, one concerned with academic matters and the intellectual approach, the other rather flippant and cavalier in manner, but committed to his craft and turning out marvellous designs, apparently effortlessly, which delighted both professionals and laymen alike. Blomfield recognised this and was willing to allow that Lutyens was 'the cleverest architect of his time'.[8] This is something of an admission, for Blomfield was usually unwilling to either praise contemporary figures, or to concede that anyone could be superior to himself. It was, no doubt, salutory for him to recognise a natural talent for design, which he could not hope to match, in the work of a man so determinedly unacademic. Symptomatically, Lutyens came to classicism much later than Blomfield. One feels that he was not concerned with any theoretical or practical reasons for using the classical language, merely that it gave him a rather different set of rules for an exciting new game of architecture, a game that he played brilliantly. Meanwhile, Blomfield had conscien-

98 The Memorial at Thiepval by Sir Edwin Lutyens

tiously researched the background and argued the case for classicism over a long period of time. He had then gone on to produce some respectable classical buildings, only to find that, later in the day, the non-intellectual Lutyens could come along and use classicism more creatively.

The difference between the two architects is well illustrated by comparing two similar buildings: Lutyens' memorial for the missing of the Somme battlefield at Thiepval, and Blomfield's Menin Gate. Both buildings had to fulfil similar requirements, partly symbolic, partly functional, to record the names of soldiers who had died in action, but who had no known graves. Lutyens' work is an architectural *tour de force*, an abstract exercise in form and planar relationships. Here, as elsewhere, he was single-mindedly pursuing the development of his art. The monument was a vehicle for the harnessing of his creative energy. The Menin Gate, on the other hand, is the product of a cerebral artist. It is full of referential material and accepted symbolism. Futhermore, it is contextual, in that Blomfield sought to relate it to the fabric of Ypres in a way that takes into account the history of the town as well as its physical actuality. Lutyens' work seems original and stimulating, Blomfield's rather predictable and obvious, yet setting aside the relative merits of the memorials as art objects it seems likely that the Menin Gate has more overt significance for the layman and is, therefore, a very valuable and successful structure.

99 The Menin Gate

100 Blomfield's Cross seen through Luytens's arch

Lutyens is exceptional in that he is one of the greatest British architects of any time. It is worthwhile examining Blomfield's relationship to his less exalted colleagues. The conclusion to be drawn, however, is that although as individuals they may compare more than favourably in terms of single, restricted aspects of work, not one is able to match Blomfield's capacity as an all-rounder. Of his old associates in the Shaw 'family', for instance, nearly all made a mark in one way or another. Lethaby, Macartney, Newton, and Prior were formidable and distinguished in their chosen areas of endeavour.

Ernest Newton's career strangely shadowed Blomfield's, from the days of the Art Workers' Guild up to his presidency of the RIBA (1914–17) which followed on directly from that of Blomfield. Newton was a quiet and sensitive man, who was concerned mainly with domestic-scale work, which he designed in a sophisticated and under-stated neo-Georgian. It 'was of an excellent quality, refined by the fastidious taste and critical sense which he possessed in a very high degree'.[9] Despite these characteristics, and his wide interests, he lacked the aggression, leadership and oratorical powers of his friend and associate.

The same may be said of the others. Macartney made a name in domestic design, became Surveyor to the Fabric of St Paul's and, as editor of the *Architectural Review*, gave the magazine a distinctive flavour. Prior's work was idiosyncratic and original, but he rose to be Slade Professor of Fine Arts at Cambridge (1912–32) and also Master of the Art Workers' Guild (1906). Lethaby's importance is well known, especially as a writer and educationalist, though he seems to have retained his arts and crafts approach to a much greater extent than the others.

Lethaby, Macartney, Newton and Prior achieved celebrity, but although they deserve to be remembered none is as famous as C. F. A. Voysey, and a final comparison may be made by following the line adopted by the late Martin S. Briggs in his article, 'Voysey and Blomfield, A Study in Contrast'.[10]

Voysey (1857–1941) and Blomfield were born and died within a year of each other. Both were members of fairly large families, the children of country clergymen.[11] Their careers began to grow at the same time, too, but here the similarities end. There were considerable differences between the two in personality, capability and outlook. Starting off within a mutual arts and crafts context – both were early members of the Art Workers' Guild – they grew apart in artistic terms, and although they must have met on occasions, there is no evidence that they knew each other well, and it is hard to believe that after about 1900 either would have found any common ground with the other.

Voysey's father was a man of strong principle, as his conflict with the Anglican hierarchy, and subsequent removal from the Church of England in 1871, shows. The same trait seems to have been continued in the son, for the hallmark of Charles Voysey's statements about architecture and art seem to be founded upon a strict moral base which was both his making and undoing.

The establishment of his principles within the context of the Arts and Crafts movement in the 1880s and 1890s gave a strength to his work and enabled him to develop both his characteristic architectural style and his textile and wallpaper design. He was already prominent and accomplished at a time when Blomfield was only just beginning to make his way in the profession. Whether he welcomed this fame or not is disputable. He was very retiring, and, for instance, was reluctant to give an interview to *Studio* magazine, even when it was pointed out to him that the publication, 'was especially anxious to raise the appreciation of design'.[12] He was exceptionally puritanical, saying that 'the wish to express oneself is corrupting to the soul and intoxicating to personal vanity'![13] Blomfield was exactly opposite. He believed in the 'personal equation' of the artist and he lost no opportunity to expound his views to the widest and most influential audience.

Voysey's puritanism found its way into his designs, along with a broadly Ruskinian approach of learning from nature. 'Love of truth', he said, 'would lead us to a more candid avowal of practical constructions and check us for disguising it or the materials of which it is made'. Again, 'simplicity, sincerity, repose, directness and frankness are moral qualities as essential to good architecture as to good men'.[14] These statements may be tellingly contrasted with Blomfield's pronouncement about the dome of St Paul's.[15]

The passing years saw Voysey stubbornly sticking to his principles, and after the turn of the century, his star fell as Blomfield's rose. Unlike Blomfield, he did not have a broad education and would, perhaps, have been more adaptable if he had had better knowledge of ideas and arguments. The new classicism came into the ascendant and, especially in the case of country houses from which Voysey made his living, cottagey styles were replaced by 'Wrenaissance' and neo-Georgian designs. Gradually, Voysey retreated into print-making, while Blomfield ruled the professional roost. He was virtually forgotten until suddenly rediscovered at the beginning of the 1930s by the architects of the Modern Movement and their apologists, who hailed him as a pioneer of modern design. Voysey was aghast, expostulating that 'it has more than once been stated and printed that I was in a measure the instigator . . . of the modern movement in architecture, in some way responsible for the square box, roofless buildings we now see . . . I am sure that those who express such views have no intention of libelling me'.[16] Consequently, at the end, he again found common ground with Blomfield, in a denunciation of the Modern Movement, but it is clear that by now, both men were out of their time.

The final paragraph of Martin Briggs' article says that 'only a rash man would dare to prophesy whether future historians will regard the burly and jovial octogenarian in the billiards room of the Athenaeum [Blomfield] as a greater architect than the quiet little figure sipping his sherry in a corner of the Arts Club, and dreaming, perhaps, of the days when his work was the cynosure of half Europe'. Up to a few years ago this speculation would have seemed incredible. Voysey was regarded as a hero and Blomfield was beneath mention. Now that the time has come to take a serious look at the Edwardian period, it is not possible to discount Blomfield, such was his influence and the breadth of his activity. It is easy to see why the young architects of the 1930s should have disliked such a dogmatic father figure, and should have felt compelled to reject him. It would have been wrong if they had not done so, for there was little future left in Blomfield's approach if interpreted directly and literally. Even C. H. Reilly was forced to side with his students in this matter.[17] Blomfield's words were not without value, but his mode of architectural expression was exhausted.

Looking back now it seems that there has been an understandably strong reaction against Blomfield, which has blotted out his name from critical discussion for virtually a quarter of a century. He can no longer be ignored, and as investigation into British architecture in the early twentieth century proceeds he will undoubtedly emerge as a very important figure. He was almost a 'complete man' in the Renaissance sense, and he was most certainly the 'complete' professional. He provides an outstanding example of the successful Edwardian architect. A type that may never be seen again, he is surely a man who deserves to be celebrated.

NOTES

Chapter 1

1 E. V. Blomfield, 'A History of the Blomfield Family' (private circulation, 1951), p. 36.
2 Hardy left Arthur Blomfield's employment fourteen years before Reginald Blomfield was articled.
3 After the death of Isabella he married Elizabeth Burra, the aunt of Reginald's future wife.
4 Blomfield, 'A History of the Blomfield Family', p. 37
5 Sir Reginald Blomfield, *Memoirs of an Architect* (London, 1932), pp. 8, 4.
6 Collection of Mrs John Ryan. R. W. Macan letter to Sir R. Blomfield, 14 November 1940.
7 Blomfield, *Memoirs*, p. 36.
8 Sir Reginald Blomfield, *Richard Norman Shaw, RA, Architect, 1831–1912. A Study* (London, 1940), p. 87.
Arthur Blomfield had two sons, A. C. and C. J. Blomfield, both of whom became architects. Their work is sometimes confused with that of their cousin.
9 Peter Ferriday, *Lord Grimthorpe, 1816–1905* (London, 1957), p. 101.
10 Blomfield, *Memoirs*, p. 37.
11 *Building News*, 46 (29 February 1884), p. 326.
12 Blomfield, *Memoirs*, p. 43.
13 Collection of Mrs John Ryan. R. Phené Spiers letter to the Rev. G. J. Blomfield, 19 January 1884.
14 Many of Blomfield's sketch books are to be found in the RIBA Drawings Collection.
15 Andrew Saint, *Richard Norman Shaw* (New Haven and London, 1976), p. 34.
16 Blomfield, *Memoirs*, p. 54.
17 James Stevens Curl, 'Broxbourne's High Quality Victorian Estate', *Hertfordshire Countryside*, 32, no. 221 (September 1977), pp. 24–26 [p. 25].
18 *The Builder*, 71 (8 August 1896), p. 116.
19 This is recorded both in the *Memoirs* and *Richard Norman Shaw, RA*.
20 Blomfield, *Memoirs*, p. 55.
21 *ibid.*, pp. 72, 73.
22 Blomfield, *Richard Norman Shaw, RA*, p. 12.
23 *ibid.*, p. 100.
24 Blomfield, *Memoirs*, p. 72.
25 Blomfield, *Richard Norman Shaw, RA*, p. 111.
26 *ibid.*, p. 91.
27 Reginald Blomfield, 'The English Tradition' in *Arts and Crafts Essays by Members of the Arts and Crafts Exhibition Society* (London 1893), p. 290, cited by Robert Macleod, *Style and Society. Architectural Ideology in Britain, 1835–1914* (London, 1971), p. 107.
28 Blomfield, *Memoirs*, p. 76.
29 *ibid.*, pp. 77–78.

Chapter 2

1 Blomfield, *Memoirs*, p. 54.
2 Blomfield, *Richard Norman Shaw, RA*, p. 17.
3 'Sussex Foundries', *Portfolio*, 17 (1886), p. 159, p. 169.
'Half-Timbered Houses in the Weald of Kent and Neighbourhood', *Portfolio*, 18 (1887), p. 1, p. 39, p. 45.
'Some Architects of the English Renaissance', *Portfolio*, 19 (1888), p. 86, p. 145, p. 185.
'Inigo Jones', *Portfolio*, 20 (1889), p. 88, p. 113, p. 126.
'A Week in Somerset', *Portfolio*, 21 (1890), p. 177.
4 William Robinson, *The English Flower Garden, etc.* 4th ed. (London, 1895), p. 6.
5 The rise in popularity of the 'old-fashioned' garden is admirably chronicled in Mark Girouard's book, *Sweetness and Light : The 'Queen Anne' Movement, 1860–1900* (Oxford, 1977).
6 Reginald Blomfield, *The Formal Garden in England* (London, 1892), p. 91.
Discussion of garden design at Art Workers' Guild meetings is mentioned in Andrew Saint, *Richard Norman Shaw* (New Haven and London, 1976), p. 459, note 83.
7 Blomfield, *Memoirs*, p. 60.
8 *ibid.*, p. 61.
9 Blomfield, *The Formal Garden*, p. 236.
10 *ibid.*, pp. 1–2.
11 *ibid.*, p. 169.
12 *ibid.*, p. 236.
13 *ibid.*, p. 85.
14 *ibid.*, p. 41.
15 Betty Massingham, *Miss Jekyll. Portrait of a Great Gardener* (Newton Abbot, 1973), p. 83.
16 Blomfield, *Memoirs*, p. 79.
17 Reginald Blomfield, *A History of Renaissance Architecture in England, 1500–1800*, 2 volumes (London, 1897), I, p. 176.
18 *ibid.*, I, p. 121.
19 *ibid.*, I, p. 170.
20 *ibid.*, II, p. 221.
21 C. H. Reilly, *Representative British Architects of the Present Day* (London, 1931), p. 58.

Chapter 3

1 Blomfield, *Richard Norman Shaw, RA*, p. 54.
2 Sir John Summerson, *The Turn of the Century. Architecture in Britain around 1900*, W. A. Cargill Memorial Lecture in Fine Art (Glasgow, 1976), p. 5.
3 Blomfield, *Memoirs*, p. 84.
4 See *ibid.*, pp. 81, 82.
5 See Christopher Hussey, 'Brocklesby Park, Lincolnshire, The Seat of The Earl of Yarborough', *Country Life*, 75 (24 February 1934), pp. 192–198.
6 Blomfield, *Memoirs*, p. 84.
7 *ibid.*, pp. 84–85.
8 A history of Chequers is to be found in J. Gilbert Jenkins, *Chequers. A History of the Prime Minister's Buckinghamshire Home* (Oxford, 1967).
9 'Apethorpe Hall, Northamptonshire, The Seat of Mr Leonard Brassey', *Country Life*, 25 (27 March, 1909), p. 450.
10 See, for instance, *The Builder*, 95 (3 October 1908), p. 352; and *Country Life*, 27 (12 March 1910), p. 378.
11 See, *The Builder*, 105 (10 October 1913), p. 370.
12 There is a discussion of the planning of Wittington in Jill Franklin, *The Gentleman's Country House and its Plan, 1835–1914* (London, 1981), p. 171. See also *The Builder*, 86 (1904), pp. 198, 223.
13 Alfred J. Burrows, *Illustrated Particulars, Plan and Conditions of Sale of Saltcote Place*, June 1920.

14 *The Builder*, 85 (14 November 1903), pp. 492–493.
15 See Note 5.
16 Blomfield, *Memoirs*, p. 83.
17 For Godinton, see *Country Life*, 21 (11 May 1907), pp. 666–673; for Knowlton, see *Country Life*, 39 (29 April 1916), pp. 534–540.

Chapter 4
1 Blomfield resigned from The Art Workers' Guild, for instance, in 1903. He had become Honorary Secretary of the Guild in 1892, but he relinquished the position in 1895 after a disagreement with the committee.
2 Blomfield, *Memoirs*, p. 61.
3 Basil H. Jackson, editor, *Recollections of Thomas Graham Jackson, Bart., RA etc. 1835–1924* (London, New York, Toronto, 1950), p. 224.
4 *ibid.*, p. 224.
5 R. Norman Shaw, editor, 'Protest Against the Examination and Registration of Architects', *The Times* (3 March 1891). The 'Memorial' was reproduced in *Architecture : A Profession or an Art?* See Note 6 below.
6 Richard Norman Shaw and T. G. Jackson, editors, *Architecture : A Profession or an Art? Thirteen Short Essays on the Qualification and Training of Architects* (London, 1892). R. Phené Spiers, Blomfield's old tutor, originally signed the Memorial, but did not wish his name to appear in the volume.
7 *ibid.*, pp. 190–191.
8 Widespread discontent with the pupilage system was voiced during the 1890s. See J. A. Gotch, editor, *The Growth and Work of the Royal Institute of British Architects, 1834–1934* (London, 1934).
9 Reginald Blomfield, 'On Architectural Education', in *Journal of the RIBA*, 12 (25 February 1905), pp. 237–245.
10 Reilly, *Scaffolding in the Sky*, pp. 214–215.
11 G. Berkeley Wills, Obituary of Sir Reginald Blomfield, *Journal of the RIBA*, 97 (January, 1943), pp. 65–67 [pp. 66–67].
12 G. Berkeley Wills, letter to author, August 1976.

13 Blomfield, *Memoirs*, pp. 107–108, quoting the resolution of the meeting, November 1905.
14 *ibid.*, p. 114.
15 See, for instance, 'Architectural Training: The Atelier', in *Journal of the RIBA*, 20 (10 May 1913), p. 493.
16 Blomfield, *Memoirs*, p. 128.
17 See note 15.
18 Blomfield, *Memoirs*, p. 153.
19 *ibid.*, p. 158.
20 See, for instance, 'Statutory Registration of Architects. Report and Recommendations of the Council', *Journal of the RIBA*, 21 (6 December 1913), pp. 80–92.
21 Blomfield restored and remodelled Leasam House, near Rye, for Admiral Sir George Warrender (1904). Warrender's wife, Lady Maude, was a well-known socialite.
22 Reginald Blomfield, *The Mistress Art* (London, 1908).
23 Blomfield, *Memoirs*, p. 112.
24 Although Blomfield was appointed in 1906, his term as Professor lasted officially from 1907 to 1911. The next Professor was A. E. Richardson, appointed in 1946.
25 Blomfield, *The Mistress Art*, p. 30.
26 *ibid.*, pp. 15–16, 139.
27 *ibid.*, pp. 157, 167, 294–295.
28 *ibid.*, pp. 42–43, 69.
29 *ibid.*, pp. 103, 104–105.
30 See C. H. Reilly, *Representative British Architects of the Present Day* (London, 1931), p. 61.
31 Blomfield was one of the original members of the editorial board of the *Architectural Review*.

Chapter 5
1 See, for example, Hill Side, Sussex, in *The Builder*, 66 (13 January 1894), p. 34.
2 Blomfield, *Memoirs*, p. 93.
3 The *ad hoc* nature of the building is emphasised by the fact that it is said that there are not two bath or wash basin taps the same in Point Hill.
4 Blomfield, *Memoirs*, p. 95.
5 The competition, judged by Norman Shaw, was won by Gerald Horsley, another member of the Shaw 'family'. See Blomfield, *Richard Norman Shaw, RA*, p. 73.

6 See *The Builder*, 72 (13 February 1897), p. 149; 106 (8 May 1914), p. 560.
7 British Architectural Library, RIBA, London, Giles Gilbert Scott papers, letter to Scott from Sir Reginald Blomfield, 8 March 1929.
8 See A. B. Gourlay, *History of Sherborne School* (Sherborne, 1971), pp. 295–300.
9 Illustrated in *Architectural Review*, 10 (October 1901), pp. 156–159. Blomfield was the Army and Navy Co-operative Society's architect, until superseded by Sir Aston Webb & Son.
10 The vulgar and overworked façade of the London County and Westminster Bank in Glasshouse Street, London (1910) must be regarded as a temporary lapse of taste. See Supplement to the *Architects' and Builders' Journal*, 38 (10 December 1913).
11 *The Builder*, 79 (3 November 1900), pp. 379–381.
12 *Architects' and Builders' Journal*, 32 (7 September 1910).
13 Blomfield designed interiors and a new staircase for the Oxford and Cambridge Club between 1906 and 1912. In 1923, he began work on the Carlton Club (see Chapter 6). The United University Club is illustrated in the Supplement to the *Architects' and Builders' Journal*, 32 (6 July 1910).
14 See John Newman, *The Buildings of England : North and East Kent* (Harmondsworth, 1969) p. 381. The church is said to be 'in the best tradition of anti-scrape'.
15 See Ian Nairn and Nikolaus Pevsner, *The Buildings of England : Surrey* (Harmondsworth, 1971), p. 344.

Chapter 6
1 Blomfield describes the misunderstanding over Delhi in the *Memoirs*. Their publication, in 1932, led Lutyens to write to Blomfield about the matter (letter in collection of Mrs John Ryan, 14 November 1932).
2 Blomfield's appointment dated officially from 1 April 1918. He resigned on 31 March 1920.

3 The example of Forceville was judged by the Commission to be the most successful, though Blomfield claims that Le Tréport was the prototype.
4 Blomfield, *Memoirs*, p. 176.
5 This was not a name chosen by Blomfield himself.
6 Blomfield, *Memoirs*, p. 179.
7 Philip Longworth, *The Unending Vigil : A History of the Commonwealth War Graves Commission* (London, 1967), p. 37.
8 Blomfield, *Memoirs*, p. 178.
9 War Memorials at Bath and Rye are examples. A grandiose project at Leeds was abandoned through lack of funds.
10 C. H. Reilly, *Representative British Architects of the Present Day* (London, 1931), p. 61.
11 Blomfield, *Memoirs*, p. 185.
12 *ibid.*, p. 187.
13 *ibid.*, p. 187. There is also a description of the foundations in *The Builder*, 126 (11 January 1924), pp. 72–75, 126–137.
14 *ibid.*, p. 188.
15 Quoted in Longworth, *The Unending Vigil*, p. 104.
16 Blomfield, *Memoirs*, p. 190.
17 *ibid.*, p. 189.
18 The history of Regent Street has been documented by Hermione Hobhouse in *A History of Regent Street* (London, 1975).
19 Blomfield, *Memoirs*, p. 212.
20 A similar scheme was put forward in 1910 by John Murray, Surveyor to the Commissioner of Woods and Forests, who proposed that it should be called King Edward VII Square. This scheme, too, was rejected and forgotten.
21 R. Norman Shaw, letter to George Leveson-Gower, Commissioner of Woods and Forests, 1 March 1912 quoted in Blomfield, *Richard Norman Shaw, RA*, p. 63.
22 Blomfield, *Memoirs*, p. 214. There had, meantime, been a competition organised by *The Builder*, for the completion of the Quadrant. It was won by Richardson and Gill, but nothing came of it. Illustrations in *The Builder*, 106 (23 January, 1914), pp. 100–102.
23 Blomfield, *Richard Norman Shaw, RA*, p. 65.

24 The general layout drawings and some $\frac{1}{2}''$ details are dated 1917, although many details were revised later on.
25 Blomfield, *Memoirs*, p. 214.
26 *ibid.*, p. 215.
27 *ibid.*, pp. 214–215.
28 A. Trystan Edwards, *Good and Bad Manners in Architecture* (London, 1924), pp. 75–76.
29 *The Builder*, 132 (24 June 1927), p. 1000.
30 Blomfield, *Memoirs*, p. 212.
31 See Trystan Edwards, *Good and Bad Manners*, p. 87.
32 The Shaftesbury Avenue – Glasshouse Street angle was to be cut off, and the segments of the Circus to the south, at the junction with Lower Regent Street, were to be replaced by stepped angles to the buildings on either side.
33 Rebuilding was again mooted in 1958 and Austin Blomfield suggested that his father's scheme should be used. No action was taken.
34 Blomfield had been architect for an abortive war memorial scheme. This was illustrated in *The Builder*, 121 (1 July 1921), p. 13.
35 Collection of Mrs John Ryan: 'Agreement of Service' between Sir Reginald Blomfield and the Corporation of the City of Leeds, 4 December 1925.
36 Leeds Corporation brochure, offering the 'island' site in the Headrow for sale.
37 *Yorkshire Post*, 4 November 1932.
38 *The Municipal Journal*, Supplement (16 October 1931).
39 *Architect and Building News*, 123 (3 January 1930), pp. 14–19 [p. 14]. It is interesting to note that Frank Scarlett, the winner of the competition, had built a house in the Modern Movement style near Rye, a few years earlier.
40 *ibid.*, p. 16.
41 Illustrated in *The Architect*, 109 (4 May 1923), p. 310. The building was destroyed by a bomb in 1940.
42 This building is no longer Barker's Store. It is illustrated in *The Builder*, 131 (3 December, 1926), pp. 903–904.

43 A description is included in *The Builder*, 132 (3 June 1927), p. 886.

Chapter 7

1 The Chantrey Bequest and other Academy matters are dealt with in Sir Walter R. M. Lamb, *The Royal Academy. A Short History of its Foundation and Development* (London, 1935), 1951).
2 Reginald Blomfield, *A History of French Architecture from the Reign of Charles VIII till the Death of Mazarin, 1494–1661*, 2 volumes (London, 1911); *A History of French Architecture from the Death of Mazarin till the Death of Louis XV, 1661–1774*, 2 volumes (London, 1921). The work is dedicated to Richard Norman Shaw, RA 'in admiration of his genius and example'.
A condensed popular version, *Three Hundred Years of French Architecture 1494-1794*, appeared in 1936.
3 *ibid.* (1911), 1, p. viii.
4 *ibid.* (1911), 1, p. 90; 2, p. 55; 1, p. 93; 1, p. 38.
5 *ibid.* (1921), 2, p. 1.
6 Sir Reginald Blomfield, *Six Architects* (London, 1935). The architects discussed are Palladio, Bernini, Jones, Mansart, Gabriel and Wren.
7 Blomfield's letter to *The Times*, 21 November 1924, was entitled 'A Dangerous Measure'. It described in detail the workings of the Metropolitan Benefices Board and also the Academy Conference. A *Times* leader was written in support of the letter and made a case for the retention of the City churches.
8 Collection of Mrs John Ryan. Sir Reginald Blomfield's private papers.
9 The questions were:
  i Do you consider Carlton Gardens and Carlton House Terrace should be demolished? If not, why not?
  ii Do you consider that the erection on the site of No. 4, Carlton Gardens of a Portland Stone building, half as high again as the original Terrace, is calculated to improve the amenities of the neighbourhood?

iii What do you think of the arguments put forward by the Commissioners of Crown Lands to justify their destruction of Carlton Gardens and Carlton House Terrace?

10 Osbert Burdett, 'Carlton House Terrace: The Chance for the Defence', in *Architectural Review*, 73 (January–June 1933), p. 49.

11 Blomfield, *Memoirs*, p. 241.

12 In 1916 Blomfield and his colleagues were vehemently against the railway bridge, but when proposing his suspension bridge, which relied on the continued presence of the railway bridge, he told the Commission: 'In my opinion as an artist . . . the railway bridge was an honest piece of engineering . . . and a coat of paint would do wonders.'

13 In a letter to *The Times*, 27 February 1925, Blomfield corrected Sir Martin Conway's suggestion that Waterloo Bridge could be rebuilt at Lambeth.

14 Sir Reginald Blomfield, *The Touchstone of Architecture* (London, 1925), 'The Bridges of London'.

15 Blomfield, *Richard Norman Shaw, RA*, pp. 100–101.

16 Blomfield, *Memoirs*, p. 248.

17 In the 1925 version, the centre span was 150 feet and those on either side 146 feet and 124 feet respectively. The built version has spans of 165 feet, 149 feet and 125 feet. The road is 36 feet wide and the footways 12 feet wide.

18 *Daily Sketch*, 8 July 1932.

19 Illustrated in the *Architect and Building News*, 121 (3 May 1929), p. 575.

Chapter 8

1 Sir Reginald Blomfield, *Modernismus* (London, 1934).

2 This address is included in *The Touchstone of Architecture*, Chapter 4.

3 Blomfield, *Memoirs*, p. 80.

4 'The New Architecture', for example, delivered at the Royal Academy, November 1930.

5 The Germanisation is used ironically.

6 Blomfield, *Modernismus*, preface.

7 Sir Reginald Blomfield and A. D. Connell, 'For and Against Modern Architecture', *The Listener*, 12 (28 November 1934), pp. 885–888 [p. 886]. This is the report of a radio debate between Blomfield and Connell.

8 Blomfield, *Modernismus*, pp. 52, 12, 13.

9 *ibid.*, p. 61 and Blomfield and Connell, *The Listener*, p. 888.

10 *ibid.*, p. 886.

11 Blomfield, *Modernismus*, pp. 71–72.

12 *ibid.*, pp. 58–59.

13 *ibid.*, p. 77.

14 C. H. Reilly, *Scaffolding in the Sky* (London, 1938), pp. 214–215.

15 Blomfield, *Richard Norman Shaw, RA*, p. 32.

16 Blomfield, *Modernismus*, p. 76.

17 *ibid.*, p. 165.

18 Blomfield's involvement with the Central Electricity Board is mentioned in Leslie Hannah, *Electricity Before Nationalisation* (London, 1979). See also S. Rowland Pierce, 'Electricity in the Landscape', *Architects' Journal*, 68 (15 August 1928), pp. 214–215.

19 He felt particularly antipathetic towards the 1935 Royal Academy Winter Exhibition, 'Art in Industry'.

20 *The Times*, 23 June 1936.

21 See, for example, a letter to *The Daily Telegraph*, 4 March 1937, about a proposal to erect a new concrete and glass house by Serge Chermayeff near Uckfield in Sussex.

22 *Evening Standard*, 31 July 1937.

23 Blomfield, *Richard Norman Shaw, RA*, preface, p. v; p. 29.

24 Ironically, he had been instrumental in the implementation of this rule.

25 British Architectural Library, RIBA, Lutyens Family Papers, LUE 21/4/1–16, 1 : 222, letter from Sir Edwin to Lady Lutyens, 23 February 1942. This attack may have been at one of the meetings of the Academy Planning Committee, in which architect members of the Academy discussed London's possible post-war redevelopment.

26 Collection of Mrs John Ryan, Sir Reginald Blomfield's private papers.

Evaluation

1 A. Trystan Edwards, letter, *Journal of the RIBA*, 97 (February 1943), p. 88.

2 Professor A. E. Richardson, Obituary of Sir Reginald Blomfield, *Journal of the RIBA*, 97 (January 1943), pp. 65–67 [pp. 65–66].

3 *ibid.*

4 G. Berkeley Wills, Obituary of Sir Reginald Blomfield, *Journal of the RIBA*, 97 (January 1943), pp. 65–67 [pp. 66–67].

5 Author's conversation with family

6 W. Curtis Green, Obituary of Sir Reginald Blomfield, *Journal of the RIBA*, 97 (January 1943), pp. 65–67 [p. 66]. A gardener at Point Hill said that he could be heard swearing from one end of the garden to the other.

7 Alastair Service, *Edwardian Architecture and Its Origins* (London 1975), p. 8.

8 Sir Reginald Blomfield, 'Epilogue 1932–1942', unpublished private manuscript.

9 Sir Reginald Blomfield, Obituary of Ernest Newton, *Journal of the RIBA*, 29 (February 1922), p. 191.

10 Martin S. Briggs 'Voysey and Blomfield, A Study in Contrast', *The Builder*, 176 (14 January 1949), pp. 39–42.

11 Blomfield was one of eleven children; Voysey one of seven.

12 *Studio*, 1 (1893), pp. 231–237 [p. 232].

13 C. F. A. Voysey, 'Self Expression in Art', *Journal of the RIBA*, 30 (10 February 1923), p. 211.

14 C. F. A. Voysey, *Individuality* (London, 1915) and 'The English house', *British Architect*, 75 (27 January 1911), p. 69.

15 See p. 43.

16 C. F. A. Voysey, letter, *Architects' Journal*, 81 (14 March 1935), p. 408.

17 Reilly, *Scaffolding in the Sky*, pp. 214–215.

APPENDIX I

Sir Reginald Blomfield: Biographical Chart

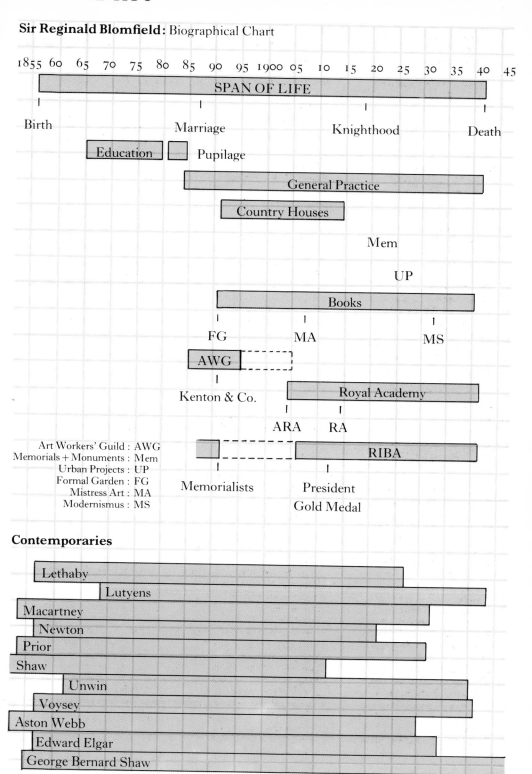

1855 60 65 70 75 80 85 90 95 1900 05 10 15 20 25 30 35 40 45

SPAN OF LIFE

Birth   Marriage   Knighthood   Death

Education   Pupilage

General Practice

Country Houses

Mem

UP

Books

FG   MA   MS

AWG

Kenton & Co.

Royal Academy

ARA   RA

Art Workers' Guild : AWG
Memorials + Monuments : Mem
Urban Projects : UP
Formal Garden : FG
Mistress Art : MA
Modernismus : MS

RIBA

Memorialists   President

Gold Medal

Contemporaries

Lethaby

Lutyens

Macartney

Newton

Prior

Shaw

Unwin

Voysey

Aston Webb

Edward Elgar

George Bernard Shaw

APPENDIX 2

Lists of Buildings

The list of works published by Austin Blomfield in the *Journal of the RIBA*, 97 (February, 1943), pp. 88–89, has been taken as the basis for this compilation. Its length and diversity indicate the scope of Blomfield's practice, and it is a useful guide for the scholar. Unfortunately, it has been found to be inaccurate in several respects and many of the smaller buildings noted have been difficult to trace. Some of the information has been rectified, but vague references which have been impossible to substantiate have been omitted.

Buildings have been listed under the following headings:
A   Domestic Work, p. 168
B   Educational and Institutional Buildings, p. 170
C   Public Buildings, p. 171
D   Clubs, p. 171
E   Commercial Buildings, p. 172
F   Ecclesiastical Work, p. 172
G   Memorials and Monuments, p. 173
H   Unrealised Projects and Competitions, p. 174

Dates shown refer to the beginnings of projects. Where building took place in a number of phases over a period of years then the date of the final phase is also given.
'Counties' refer to those in existence before April 1974, which are similar to those in Blomfield's lifetime.

A · Domestic Work
Listed aphabetically according to the name of the house or location.

Name	*Location*	*Work*	*Date*
Apethorpe Hall	Apethorpe, Northamptonshire	Alterations & Additions to House & New Gardens	1904
Ballard's Court	Goudhurst, Kent	House	1903
Blacknoll	Dorset	House	1889
Borrowstone Lodge	Kincardine O'Neil, Aberdeenshire	House	1893
Brandfold	Goudhurst, Kent	Stables & Alterations	1895
Brocklesby Park	Brocklesby, Lincolnshire	Reconstruction, Alterations & Gardens	1899
Brodick Castle	Isle of Arran	Gardens & Restoration	1919
Brooklands	Weybridge, Surrey	Alterations & Renovation	1889
20 Buckingham Gate (formerly James St)	London	House	1887
Cadboro	Rye, Sussex	Pair of Cottages	1890
Caythorpe Court	Caythorpe, Lincolnshire	House & Gardens	1899
Chequers Court	Nr Wendover, Buckinghamshire	Gardens, Restoration & Alterations	1892, 1909
Chicheley	Newport Pagnell, Buckinghamshire	House	1902
Cowley House	Cowley, Middlesex	Alterations	1896
Crockerhill	Crockerhill, Sussex	Alterations	1929
Culverthorpe Hall	Culverthorpe, Lincolnshire	Alterations	1900
Ditton Place	Balcombe, Sussex	Gardens	1900
Drakelow Hall	Burton-upon-Trent, Derbyshire	Gardens & Restoration	1906
Elfordleigh House	Nr Plymouth, Devon	House	1899

Euston Hall	Suffolk	Gardens	1902
Foynes Village	Foynes, Ireland	8 Houses	1890,
			1924
Friars	Winchelsea, Sussex	Alterations & Restoration	1912
Frogmore Hall	Frogmore,	Alterations	1892
	Hertfordshire		
Nos. 49, 51, Frognal	Hampstead, London	Pair of Houses	1892
Garnons	Mansell Gammage,	Alterations	1907
	Herefordshire		
Godinton Park	Ashford, Kent	Alterations & Garden	1895,
		Design	1920
Gogmagog Hall	Nr Cambridge	Alterations	1903
Halstead Hall	Stixwould,	Restoration	1922
	Lincolnshire		
Hammonds	Udimore, Sussex	Alterations	1906
Harefield Place	Nr Uxbridge,	Alterations	1920
	Middlesex		
Hatchlands	Nr Guildford, Surrey	The Music Room	1902
Heathfield Park	Heathfield, Sussex	Alterations & Additions	1896
Hill Hall	Theydon Mount,	Alterations & Additions	1909
	Essex		
Hill House	Shenley, Herts	Gardens	1907
Hillside	Hurst Green, Sussex	House	1892
Houses of Rest	Hucknall,	6 'Houses of Rest for Miners'	1925
	Nottinghamshire		
Kenfield Hall	Petham, Kent	Alterations	1906
Kent House	Knightsbridge,	Decorations & Internal	1909
	London	Alterations (Concert Room)	
Kingsbury	Kingsbury, London	Concrete House	1926
Knowlton Court	Knowlton, Kent	Alterations & Gardens	1904
Leasam	Nr Rye, Sussex	Alterations to House & New	1903
		Gardens	
Lockleys	Welwyn,	Alterations, Additions &	1911
	Hertfordshire	New Gardens	
The Lordship	Much Hadham,	Additions	1912
	Hertfordshire		
Lyveden	Northamptonshire	Restoration	1909
Manoire de la	Jersey	Restoration & Additions	1909
Trinité			
Mellerstain	Kelso, Roxburghshire	Restoration & Gardens	1898
Milner Court (Sturry	Sturry, Kent	Additions & Gardens	1907
Court)			
Moundsmere Manor	Nutley, Hampshire	House & Gardens	1908
Murraythwaite	Dumfries, Dumfries-	House	1901
	shire		
Mystole	Chartham, Kent	Alterations & Additions	1895
Netherseale Hall	Nr Ashby-de-la-	Restoration	1914
	Zouche, Derbyshire		
Norton Court	Faversham, Kent	Restoration	1910
Old Mansion	Boldre, Hampshire	House & Gardens	1902
Packer's Close	Newbury, Berkshire	House	1913

Penn House	Amersham, Buckinghamshire	Alterations	1918
Penn House	Bath, Somerset	Remodelling	1904
Point Hill	Playden, Rye, Sussex	Development of Old Cottage	1895
Point Hill (Lavender Walk, The Point, Point House, Point Lodge, The Croft)	Playden, Rye, Sussex	Houses	1899
Robbins House	New York, USA	House	1900
Rye, Gun Garden and Watchbell Street	Rye, Sussex	Houses	1890, 1910
St Catherine's Estate	Broxbourne, Hertfordshire	5 Houses	1887
Saltcote Place	Rye, Sussex	House	1905
Sandwich Bay	Sandwich, Kent	Houses	1912
Sheerwater Estate	Byfleet, Surrey	Houses	1890
Southwater	Horsham, Sussex	House & Gardens	1891
Sulgrave Manor	Sulgrave, Northamptonshire	Additions & Restoration	1921
Swinford Old Manor	Nr Ashford, Kent	Restoration	1887
Swiftsden	Hurst Green, Sussex	House	1892
20 Upper Grosvenor Street	London	Alterations & Redecoration	1910
Waldershare Park	Waldershare, Kent	Refitting after fire	1914
Wandsworth Trust	Long Sutton, Hampshire	Houses & Cottages	1915
Warley Lodge	Warley, Essex	Gardens	1894
West Broyle	Chichester, Sussex	House	1901
Westwood Park	Worcestershire	Restoration of Roofs	1924
Whiteley Village	Surrey	Houses (various architects designed buildings for Whiteley Village Homes)	1911
Wittington	Medmenham, Buckinghamshire	House & Gardens	1897, 1909
Woodcote Manor	Bramdean, Hampshire	Additions & Alterations	1911
Wretham Hall	Wretham, Norfolk	House & Gardens	1912
Wyphurst	Cranleigh, Surrey	Extensive Additions	1907
Yockley	Frimley, Surrey	House & Gardens	1901

B · Educational and Institutional Buildings

Listed alphabetically according to the name of the institution.

Name	Location	Work	Date
Blundell's School	Tiverton, Devon	Additions	1901
British School	Ypres, Belgium	New Building	1925
Felsted School	Essex	Boarding House	1900
Goldsmith's College	New Cross, London	Art School	1907
Haileybury College	Nr Hertford	Bradby Memorial Hall, Music School, Sports Pavilion, Organ Case	1886, 1923
Hillside School	Goldalming, Surrey	School Buildings & House	1897

Lady Margaret Hall	Oxford	College Buildings	1896
		Wordsworth	1909
		Talbot	1914
		Toynbee	1926
Lord Wandsworth Agricultural College	Long Sutton, Hampshire	Farm Buildings, Lodge & Entrance Gates (Main Building by E. Guy Dawber)	1913
Queen Anne's School	Caversham, Berkshire	Chapel	1893
Sherborne School	Dorset	Carrington Building, North Court, Gymnasium, Music School	1894, 1926
St Edmund's School	Canterbury, Kent	Head Master's House	1897

C · Public Buildings
Listed alphabetically according to location.

Name	Location	Work	Date
Holburne Museum	Bath	Conversion & Alterations	1911
Covered Market	Hertford	New Building (with W. H. Wilds)	1889
Public Library & Art School	Hertford	New Building (with W. H. Wilds)	1889
Old County Hall (Newcastle House)	Lewes, Sussex	Extension & Restoration	1930
Public Library	Lincoln	New Building	1910
Usher Gallery	Lincoln	New Building	1927
Water Tower	Lincoln	New Building	1910
Gray's Inn Hall	London	Panelling	1914
Lambeth Bridge	London	New Building	1925, 1932
Merchant Taylors' Hall	London	Alterations	1904, 1926
Middlesex Hospital	London	New Façade	1930
Royal College of Physicians	London	Restoration & Decoration	1910
Cottage Hospital	Playden, Rye, Sussex	New Building	1921
Water Tower	Playden, Rye, Sussex	New Building	1896
Parish Institute	Portsea, Portsmouth, Hampshire	New Building	1897
Chantry Bridge	Rotherham, Yorkshire	Reconstruction & Renovation	1927

In addition, Austin Blomfield notes (in the *Journal of the RIBA*) a public building, Rhoades House, New York, 1912, which has not been traced.

D · Clubs
Listed alphabetically according to the name of the club.

Name	Location	Work	Date
Carlton Club	Pall Mall, London	Refacing of Original Building & Extension	1920

Oxford & Cambridge Club	Pall Mall, London	Alterations, including Staircase	1906
United University Club	Suffolk St, London	New Building & Extensions	1906, 1924, 1938

E · Commercial Buildings

Listed alphabetically according to the name of the scheme.

Name	Location	Work	Date
Amen Corner	London	Shops & Offices	1900
Army & Navy Stores	London	Restaurant	1913
Army & Navy Stores	Greycoat Place, London	Warehouse	1895
John Barker's Stores	Kensington High Street, London	Design of Elevations	1924
No 4 Carlton Gardens	London	Offices	1932
Central Electricity Board		'Pylons'	1927
Davies Mews, South Moulton St.	London	Offices, Storerooms & Stables	1901
Drummonds Bank (opposite)	Charing Cross, London	Additional Building	1914
Headrow & Associated Development	Leeds	New Street, with Shops, Offices & Banks, etc. (in conjunction with other architects, notably G. W. Atkinson).	1924, 1937
Kinnaird House	Pall Mall	New Building (with A. J. Driver)	1915
London & County Bank, King's Road	Chelsea, London	New Building	1909
London, County & Westminster Bank	Glasshouse Street, London	New Building	1910
Regent Street. Quadrant & Part Piccadilly Re-development	London	Redevelopment of Street with New Shops and Stores	1916, 1926

F · Ecclesiastical Work

Listed alphabetically according to town or parish.

Name	Location	Work	Date
Aldington, St Martin's	Aldington, Kent	Panelling & Lychgate	1906
Beckley Church	Beckley, Sussex	Restoration & Additions	1888, 1925
Berne, St Antonien Kapelle	Berne, Switzerland	Rebuilding of Church	1891
Boxford, Church	Boxford, Suffolk	Restoration	1886
Carshalton, All Saints'	Carshalton, Surrey	Church Plate & Extension (with A. W. Blomfield)	1891

172

Name	Location	Work	Date
Chingford, Church of St Peter and St Paul	Chingford Green, Essex	Chancel	1903
Farnham Church	Farnham, Surrey	Pulpit	1898
Ickenham Church	Ickenham, Suffolk	Restoration	1890
Ivychurch, St George's	Ivychurch, Kent	Restoration	1888
Launton Church	Launton, Oxfordshire	Restoration	1890
Lavant Church	Lavant, Chichester, Sussex	Pulpit, Organ Case	1895, 1926
Limpsfield, St Peter's	Limpsfield, Surrey	Lychgate	1899
Limpsfield Chart, St Andrew's	Limpsfield Chart, Surrey	New Buildings	1895, 1902
St James's Church	Piccadilly, London	New Entrance Gate & Piers	1937
St Paul's Cathedral	London	Processional Cross	1897
Molash, St Peter's	Molash, Kent	Restoration	1895
Newstead Vicarage	Newstead, Lincs	Vicarage	1919
Portslade, St Andrew's	Portslade, Sussex	Alterations & Additions	1890
The Monastery	Rye, Sussex	Restoration	1909
Vicarage, Mission Room	Rye, Sussex	New Buildings	1887, 1900
Warnham Church	Warnham, Sussex	Restoration	1886
West Grinstead Church	West Grinstead, Sussex	Design for New Church	1889
Writtle Church	Writtle, Essex	Church Restoration	1892
Ypres, St George's	Ypres, Belgium	New Memorial Church (with Austin Blomfield)	1928

G · Memorials and Monuments

Listed alphabetically according to location, except where the monument has a specific name.

Name	Location	Work	Date
Aldington Church	Kent	Memorials	1906
Abbots Langley, War Memorial	Hertfordshire	Memorial	1919
Anson Memorial	All Soul's College, Oxford	Paving & Memorial	1911
Bath War Memorial	Avon	Memorial	1923
Belgian War Memorial	Victoria Embankment, London	Memorial	1917
J. E. Blomfield, M.D., Memorial	Magdalen College, Oxford	Memorial	1921
Bury War Memorial	Lancashire	Memorial	1924
Elm Green War Memorial	Danbury, Essex	Memorial	1921
Eltham War Memorial	London	Memorial	1919
Haileybury College War Memorials	Hertfordshire	Memorials	1903, 1923
Hertfordshire Regiment Memorial	All Saints' Church, Hertford	Memorial	1921
Howard Memorial	Glossop, Derbyshire	Memorial	1919
Kilkenny Church	Co. Kilkenny, Ireland	Memorial Reredos	undated
Kitchener Memorial	London	Memorial	1921

Limerick War Memorial	Co. Limerick, Ireland	Memorial	1923
Lincoln War Memorial	Lincoln	Memorial	1923
War Memorial London	Sloane Square, London	Memorial	c. 1920
War Memorial, Loch Shiel	Lochaber, Inverness-shire	Memorial	1919
Lord Cawley Memorial	Church of St Peter and St Paul, Eye, Hertfordshire	Memorial	1919
Luton War Memorial	Bedfordshire	Memorial	1921
Menin Gate	Ypres, Belgium	Memorial	1922
Northfleet War Memorial	Kent	Memorial	1923
Old Buckenham War Memorial	Norfolk	Memorial	c. 1920
Royal Air Force Memorial	Embankment, London	Memorial	1921
Rye War Memorial	Sussex	Memorial	1921
St Paul's Cross	St Paul's Cathedral, London	Monument	1910
Torquay War Memorial	Devon	Memorial	1921
Ware War Memorial	Hertfordshire	Memorial	undated
Yarborough Memorial	Brocklesby Church, Lincolnshire	Memorial to Countess of Yarborough	1926

In addition there is a drawing (in the RIBA Drawings Collection) showing a wall-mounted memorial to Lord Roberts, but with no indication of place or date.

Work for the Imperial War Graves Commission includes the design of the War Cross and cemeteries in association with junior architects.

H · Unrealised Projects and Competitions
Listed alphabetically by name.

Name	Location	Work	Date
Carlton House Terrace	London	Total Redevelopment	1933
Charing Cross Bridge	London	New Suspension Bridge	1930
Eyot Bridge	Shepperton	New Bridge	1921
Piccadilly Circus	London	Overall Redevelopment	1929
St Paul's School for Girls	London, Hammersmith	Competition	1896
Strand (Aldwych)	London	Competition	1900
Stratford-upon-Avon Bridge	Stratford	New Bridge	1928
Waterloo Bridge	London	Widening	1926, 1932
War Memorial	Leeds	Memorial	1920

BIBLIOGRAPHY

1 Unpublished Material

Blomfield, E. V., 'A History of the Blomfield Family', 1951. Copies in possession of family.

Blomfield, Sir Reginald, 'Epilogue, 1932–1942', 1942. Copy in possession of family.

Blomfield family collection (Mrs John Ryan and Mr Paul Blomfield, London): Correspondence, business documents, photographs.

British Architectural Library, RIBA, London:
Papers of J. N. Comper; Sir Walter Lamb; Lutyens family; Sir Edward Maufe; A. Beresford Pite; Sir Giles Gilbert Scott; J. O. Scott; Harry Sirr; Marshall A. Sisson.

RIBA Drawings Collection, London: Perspective and orthographic drawings of designs by Sir Reginald Blomfield; working and detail drawings of designs by Sir Reginald Blomfield and his office; perspective drawings of Blomfield's projects by others; Blomfield's sketch books; photographs, and other documents.

Sherborne School archive: Correspondence, business documents, drawings.

West Sussex Record Office, Chichester: Correspondence.

2 Published Material

i BOOKS BY BLOMFIELD, LISTED IN CHRONOLOGICAL ORDER

The Formal Garden in England. London, 1892

A History of Renaissance Architecture in England, 1500–1800. 2 volumes. London, 1897

A Short History of Renaissance Architecture in England, 1500–1800. London, 1900

Studies in Architecture. London, 1905

The Mistress Art. London, 1908

A History of French Architecture from the Reign of Charles VIII till the Death of Mazarin, 1494–1661. 2 volumes. London, 1911

Architectural Drawing and Draughtsmen. London, New York, Toronto and Melbourne, 1912

A Suffolk Family. Private publication, 1916

A History of French Architecture from the Death of Mazarin till the Death of Louis XV, 1661–1774. 2 volumes. London, 1921

The Touchstone of Architecture. London, 1925

Byways. Leaves from an Architect's Note-Book. London, 1929

Memoirs of an Architect. London, 1932

Modernismus. London, 1934

Six Architects. London, 1935

Three Hundred Years of French Architecture, 1494–1794. London, 1936

Sébastien le Prêstre de Vauban, 1633–1707. London, 1938

Richard Norman Shaw, RA, Architect, 1831–1912. A Study. London, 1940

ii SELECT LIST OF PERIODICAL ARTICLES BY BLOMFIELD
This list is by no means comprehensive, and it excludes specific references in periodicals to Blomfield's buildings which are, in any case, given in the notes.

'Sussex Foundries', *Portfolio*, 17 (1886), p. 159; p. 169

'Half-Timbered Houses in the Weald of Kent and Neighbourhood', *Portfolio*, 18 (1887), p. 1; p. 39; p. 45

'Some Architects of the English Renaissance', *Portfolio*, 19 (1888), p. 86; p. 145; p. 185

'Dordt', *English Illustrated Magazine* (February 1889), pp. 398–406

'Inigo Jones', *Portfolio*, 20 (1889), p. 88; p. 113; p. 126

'A Week in Somerset', *Portfolio*, 21 (1890), p. 177

'The Architect of Newgate', *Architectural Review*, 10 (October 1901), pp. 123–138

175

'Municipal Bodies and Architecture', *Architectural Review*, (January–June 1902), pp. 107–112

'The Italians at Fontainebleau', *Architectural Review*, 12 (June–December 1902), pp. 201–223

'Andrea Palladio', *Architectural Review*, 13 (January–June 1903), pp. 127–139

'Philibert de l'Orme', *Architectural Review*, 15 (January–June 1904), pp. 40–53, 93–105; 17 (January–June 1905), pp. 12–23

'On Architectural Education', *Journal of the RIBA*, 12 (25 February 1905), pp. 237–245

'Pierre Lescot and Jean Goujon', *Journal of the RIBA*, 18 (1910–11), pp. 109–128

'Architectural Training: The Atelier', *Journal of the RIBA*, 20 (10 May 1913), p. 493

'Christopher Wren', *Architectural Review*, 53 (January–June 1923), pp. 73–76

Blomfield, Sir Reginald & Connell, A. D., 'For and Against Modern Architecture', *The Listener*, 12 (28 November 1934), pp. 885–888

iii SECONDARY SOURCES AND OTHER WORKS USED FOR REFERENCE
An * denotes work not cited in text or footnotes.

Briggs, Martin S. 'Voysey & Blomfield, A Study in Contrast', *Builder*, 176 (14 January 1949), pp. 39–42

Burdett, Osbert, Lord Clonmore et al., 'Carlton House Terrace', *Architectural Review*, 73 (January–June 1933), pp. 8–16, 49

*Cooper, N., *The Opulent Eye. Late Victorian and Edwardian Taste in Interior Design, 1885–1914*. London, 1976

Edwards, A. Trystan, *Good and Bad Manners in Architecture*. London, 1924

Ferriday, Peter, *Lord Grimthorpe, 1816–1905*. London, 1957

Franklin, Jill, *The Gentleman's Country House and its Plan, 1835–1914*. London, 1981

Gebhard, David, *Charles F. A. Voysey, Architect*. Los Angeles, 1975

Girouard, Mark, *Sweetness and Light : The 'Queen Anne' Movement, 1860–1900*. Oxford, 1977

Gotch, J. Alfred, ed., *The Growth and Work of the Royal Institute of British Architects, 1834–1934*. London, 1934

Gourlay, A. B., *A History of Sherborne School*. Sherborne, 1971

Green, W. Curtis, Richardson, A. E. and Wills, G. Berkeley, 'Obituary of Sir Reginald Blomfield', *Journal of the RIBA*, 97 (January 1943), pp. 65–67

Hannah, Leslie, *Electricity Before Nationalisation*. London, 1979

Hobhouse, Hermione, *A History of Regent Street*. London, 1975

Hussey, Christopher, *The Life of Sir Edwin Lutyens*. London, 1953

Jackson, Basil H., ed., *Recollections of Thomas Graham Jackson, Bart., RA, etc., 1835–1924*. London, New York, Toronto, 1950

Jenkins, J. Gilbert, *Chequers, A History of the Prime Minister's Buckinghamshire Home*. Oxford, 1967

Kay, Barrington, *The Development of the Architectural Profession in Britain. A Sociological Study*. London, 1960

Lamb, Sir Walter R.M., *The Royal Academy. A Short History of its Foundation and Development*. London, 1935, 1951

Longworth, Philip, *The Unending Vigil. A History of the Commonwealth War Graves Commission*. London, 1967

*Macartney, Mervyn, E., *Recent English Domestic Architecture*. 4 volumes. London, 1908–1911

Macleod, Robert, *Style and Society. Architectural Ideology in Britain, 1835–1914*. London, 1971

Massingham, Betty, *Miss Jekyll. Portrait of a Great Gardener*. Newton Abbot, 1973

Pevsner, Sir Nikolaus, et al., *The Buildings of England*. Harmondsworth, 1951 et seq.

Reilly, C. H., *Representative British Architects of the Present Day*. London, 1931

Reilly, C. H., *Scaffolding in the Sky. A Semi-Architectural Autobiography*. London, 1938

Robinson, William, *The English Flower Garden, Design Arrangement, and Plans, Followed by A Description of all the Best Plants for it and Their Culture and the Positions fitted for Them*. London, 1883, 1895

Saint, Andrew, *Richard Norman Shaw*. New Haven and London, 1976

Service, Alastair, ed., *Edwardian Architecture and its Origins*. London, 1975

Shaw, Richard Norman and Jackson, T. G., eds., *Architecture : A Profession or an Art? Thirteen Short Essays on the Qualification and Training of Architects*. London, 1892

Summerson, Sir John, *The Turn of the Century. Architecture in Britain around 1900* (W. A. Cargill Memorial Lecture in Fine Art). Glasgow, 1976

Thompson, Paul, *The Edwardians. The Remaking of British Society*. London, 1975

Voysey, C. F. A., 'The English House', *British Architect*, 75 (27 January 1911), p. 69

Voysey, C. F. A., 'Self Expression in Art', *Journal of the RIBA*, 30 (10 February 1923), p. 211

*Watkin, David, *The Rise of Architectural History*. London, Westfield, N. J., 1980

*Weaver, L., *Small Country Houses of Today*. London, 1910

'Statutory Registration of Architects, Report and Recommendations of the Council', *Journal of the RIBA*, 21 (6 December 1913), pp. 80–92

The following periodicals were consulted for reviews and reports:
Academy Architecture ; Architect ; Architect and Building News ; Architects' Journal ; Architects' and Builders' Journal ; Architectural Review ; The Builder ; Building News ; Country Life ; The Municipal Journal.

INDEX